The GopherHaul guide on how to get customers for your landscaping and lawn care business
Volume 3.

Anyone can start a landscaping or lawn care business but the tricky part is finding customers. This book will show you how.

By Steve Low

Host of The GopherHaul Lawn Care Business Show

and the Gopher Lawn Care Business Forum.

Coming up with marketing and service ideas to keep busy and profitable all year long can be difficult. Most of the times we are just not in the mood to sit and think up creative ways to make more money.

Well thankfully I have been able to interview thousands of lawn care business owners over the years and ask them what's worked and what hasn't. The responses and the follow up questions have really uncovered a treasure trove of ideas that I compiled here to share with you.

Now you don't have to get frustrated when trying to come up with new ideas. Just keep this book around as a reference. Some of these ideas might just work right off the shelf while others might need to be altered to fit your needs. Ultimately it's always better to have ideas on stand by just in case.

Below is a thanks our friend Andy posted on the Gopher Forum for all to see. To me, this sentiment makes it all worthwhile. I know at the end of my day at least one person has been inspired to dream and not give up, because success is just right around the corner.
Dream it, Build It, Gopher It!

Sincerely, Steve

"I've been reading posts here on The Gopher Forum for a while. This site is the single biggest help with my business. No, it's the ONLY help I get with my business! I used a web template found here, used the estimation calculators, the advice and opinions are priceless, and even the moral support is needed."

Thanks for everything guys! Andy

Contents

Special thanks to Gopher Lawn Care Software.

This book would not have been possible without the help and guidance of all our friends and business owners we have met over the years on our Gopher Forum.

Also thank you to the staff at Gopher Software for making all of this possible.

Lawn Care Software
PROBLEM: Scheduling & billing repetitive jobs is tedious and time consuming.
SOLUTION: Gopher Billing & Scheduling Software allows you to Quickly and Easily schedule jobs and create invoices.

Gopher Landscape Billing and Scheduling Software simplifies the task of scheduling your lawn care jobs and billing your customers. Simply set up your jobs at the beginning of the season and let Gopher handle the rest. With Gopher, you can print out a list of scheduled jobs for each day and then automatically print invoices after those jobs have been completed.

Download your free trial of Gopher Billing & Scheduling Software at http://www.gophersoftware.com

Continue your reading.

I have more great information on running a lawn care business in my other books, "**Stop Lowballing! A Lawn Care Business Owner's Guide To Success.**"

Some of the topics discussed in the book: - How to start up your lawn care business. - Finding your niche and finding profits. - Lawn Care Equipment. - Pricing & Estimating Lawn Care Jobs. - Dealing With Customers. - Dealing With Employees. - Lawn Care Marketing Secrets. - Lawn Care Business Tips. - Getting Commercial Accounts without commercial references. - Pitfalls of Commercial Accounts. And more.

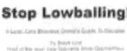

The GopherHaul Lawn Care Marketing & Landscaping Business Show Episode Guide.

Topics discuss include: How to raise start up capital. Seasonal marketing ideas. What to do when your largest client leaves? What's better to use, postcards or brochures? How to build your customer base with referrals? Gain one customer then lose one customer. How to stop it? How to pre-qualify customers when they call? How to bid jobs. What should you include in a commercial lawn care bid? What newspaper ads work best? How to buy a lawn care business. Tips on buying used lawn care equipment. And much more.

How to get customers for your landscaping and lawn care business all year long. Volume 1.

Anyone can start a lawn care business, the tricky part is finding customers. Learn how in this book.

New lawn care business owners were polled and 33% of them said the toughest part about running their business was finding customers. This book shows you how to get new lawn care customers. Don't start from scratch and try to re-create the wheel. Learn what works and what doesn't.

Volume #1 discusses: Getting started, choosing a business name, harnessing employees to sell, community marketing ideas, free rentals to offer, hosting events to get exposure, volunteer projects to build goodwill, how to get residential and commercial customers (including sample letters). Bikini lawn care, getting in your local paper, marketing on price, publicity stunts & media attention, organic lawn care marketing, reaching out to realtors, turning hobbies into marketing ideas, seasonal marketing ideas that work.

How to get customers for your landscaping and lawn care business all year long. Volume 2.

Anyone can start a lawn care business but most get stuck finding customers and they give up their new venture too quickly. Why struggle trying to learn how to gain new lawn care customers the hard way? This book gives you lawn care marketing ideas that are being used by your competitors. It also talks about what marketing ideas don't work.

Volume #2 discusses: The most effective lawn care business marketing methods. How to track your ads, the best ways to utilize: billboards, brochures, business cards, buying lawn care customers, clubs & organizations, coupons & gift cards, co-marketing, door hangers, going door to door, flyers, internet marketing, lawn signs, customer letters, direct mailing, newsletters, newspaper ad, phone book advertising, phones & telemarketing, postcards, referrals, sports, testimonials, trade shows, truck & trailer advertising, word of mouth.

The Big Lawn Care Marketing Book

This book contains 470 pages of marketing ideas to help your lawn care & landscaping business grow.

The Big Lawn Care Marketing Book contains volume 1 & 2 of my other books "How to get customers for your landscaping and lawn care business all year long."

The landscaping and lawn care business plan startup guide.

If you ever had thought about starting your own lawn care or landscaping business but weren't sure how to go about putting together a business plan, this book will show you examples of lawn care business plans created on the Gopher Lawn Care Business Forum. The author of this lawn care business book is the host of The GopherHaul Lawn Care Business Show and the Gopher Lawn Care Business Forum.

Inside is a step by step guide on how to make a landscape or lawn care business plan with real life examples including income and expense projections as well as customer acquisition goals. This lawn care business book is a great tool to help you improve your odds of finding success.

How to use Gopher Lawn Care Business Billing & Scheduling Software.

Learn how to manage your lawn care and landscaping business easier with this powerful software.

A Rebellious Teenagers Guide To Starting A Landscaping & Lawn Care Business.

When you are a teenager you have a lot of rebellious energy. Why not take that energy, harness it to be productive, and make money! This book will show you how to succeed in starting your own landscaping & lawn care business. I cover the basics of how to register your business to advanced topics like incentives to get employees to sell more.

Unfiltered, unedited, and a little rough. A collection of landscaping & lawn care business lessons I've learned along the way.

I see so many new lawn care businesses get started only to fail a short time later because the entrepreneurs didn't educate themselves enough about their field. Here is a collection of lessons I learned that will give your lawn care or landscaping business a better chance at success.

You can order these books through the following websites:

http://www.gophersoftware.com

http://www.gopherforum.com

http://www.lawnchat.com

http://www.amazon.com

Fall lawn care leaf cleanup letter also used for gutter cleaning.

One of our forum members shared with us this fall leaf clean up letter. Before Fall comes along, why not send out this letter in your invoices to your lawn care customers. Ask them how you should handle their leaf clean up and also offer other additional Fall services like gutter cleaning.

A lawn care business owner suggested when bidding out your gutter cleaning, to charge $60 per hour. This should help you when you are estimating your jobs.

Here is another way, that was shared to bid on gutter cleaning jobs. He said "You're leaving money on the table doing it by the hour.

If you are called to a residential property just for gutter clean out you should be charging by the foot and it should include down spout flushing. $1 a ft and if it's 2 story it should be a little extra for the height. ALWAYS PRACTICE SAFETY WHEN WORKING OFF LADDERS AND ON ROOFS. AN INJURY CAN TAKE YOU OUT OF THE GAME COMPLETELY, COSTING YOU MORE THAN MONEY.

If your doing a fall clean up, (leaf clean up and removal) gutter clean out should be included. Plant beds are not extra either, they are a part of the lawn.

These are common practices with-in my area."

I thought this was very interesting! So I asked, when you give a bid for a fall yard cleanup, do you include a line item that shows gutter cleaning and a price for that? Do you include another line item for plant beds? Or are all these included into one price and it isn't broken down at all?

He said "this is what I include. We here by propose to; clear all lawn and plant bed areas of leaves to the best of our ability. Clean and flush all gutters and down spouts as follows,

Fall Lawn Clean Up $X.XX
(All lawn and plant bed areas)

Gutter Clean Out $X.XX
(Cleaning and flushing all gutter & down spouts)

Total Due $X.XX

If the customer balks at the gutter charges then explain to them the importance of having them cleaned out. Most will go for it."

Here is a sample letter you could include in your invoices to help sell this service.

Dear Valued Customer,

With Fall nearly upon us, and assuming you have trees in or near your yard, leaves will soon be falling and covering your lawn. Since Fall clean-up are not included in our basic service, we need to find out how you would like to deal with leave removal.

We can either:

1. Mow as usual, mulching the leaves back into the lawn, allowing them to break down naturally at no additional charge or;

2. Rake, bag and dispose of the leaves.

If you wish to have the leaves removed, we will be happy to provide you with a free quote.

Don't forget to ask about our additional services.

  1. Gutter Cleaning
  2. Hedge Trimming
  3. Flower Bed Weeding
  4. Power Washing
  5. Brush Removal
  6. Bush Hogging
  7. Storm Cleanup

If you need a home or lawn service that's not listed, give us a call.

As always, thank you so much for your business and please call us at any time for any reason.

Sincerely,

Your Name

Owner

3 month before and after lawn care customer retention letter sample.

One important thing to remember is that most lawn care customers who are going to cancel service will cancel it shortly after signing up with you. A lawn care business owner who studied this said "when researching our cancellation history I found that most of the canceled lawn care accounts had been canceled within the first 3-4 months. If they had been more informed from the beginning, maybe we could have saved the sale."

So if we know that most customers who cancel, tend to cancel early on in the service, due to buyers remorse or a feeling of guilt from spending money on lawn service, why not stop that problem before it happens. Give the customer a good reason why they should keep having you service their yard. Show them the value they are receiving.

One way to do this would be to create a before and after customer letter that focused on a specific problem you were able to resolve. How can you do this?

- When you first sign up a new customer, take some photos of problem areas on their property.
- Within 3 months, try to resolve at least one of those specific problems and take photos of how the property looks afterwards.
- Then send a letter to the customer that shows them how you are working to resolve issues with their lawn and

show how you were able to achieve it on this specific section.

- Maybe put this letter in with your 3rd month invoice or send it separately with a special envelope that says 3 month lawn status on the back.
- Ultimately the customer will feel they are receiving value and will want to continue using your lawn care service.

Here is a lawn care customer template to help you get started with this.

Dear Customer,

3 Month Lawn Care Update.

I wanted to take a moment and thank you for choosing Joe's Lawn Service to provide you with the best lawn care available. Over these past few months I have been hard at work resolving issues your lawn was struggling with.

I have included a before and after picture of one particular troubled lawn spot that has been resolved. You can see the brown spots on the before picture and a few months later in the same area, the spots are now gone. The reason this spot was occurring was due to a brown spot fungus. Such a fungus will not go away by itself and needed to be treated.

It is my privilege to work for you and help you create that perfect lawn. If you find other problems about your yard you want address, don't hesitate to contact me through email or call my cell phone.

Regards,
Your Name

Lawn care business commercial property bid cover letter sample.

When your lawn care business is submitting a bid for commercial property maintenance, consider including this bid cover letter sample. It's a great way to look professional and improve your chances at winning the lawn care bid.

Mr. Smith
123 Main St
Anytown, USA 90210
(800) 123-4567

RE: Weekly Lawn Maintenance

Dear Mr. Smith,

Thank you for giving Joe's Lawn Care the opportunity to submit this proposal to provide you with lawn care services for your property located in CITY, STATE.

The pricing bid for this property is outlined on the enclosed quotation sheet. The cost is based on weekly mowing, trimming, edging, and blowing down of all hard surfaces. Five (5) premium fertilizing applications and a spring core aerating. If you find any of this information to be in question please give me a call at xxx-xxxx.

Again, thank you for the opportunity to submit this proposal. We are excited to establish this new business relationship. We are looking forward to doing business with you this year and we are confident you will be extremely pleased with our services.

Sincerely,

Your Name
Owner

End of the lawn care season customer letter sample.

When the lawn mowing season comes to a close you might want to consider sending your customers this end of the season lawn care letter. This is a great way to reach out to your lawn care customers and say thank you.

December 1, 20XX

Homeowner
10 Any Street
Your city, State 90210

Dear Customer,

I would like to thank you again for choosing Joe Smith Landscaping for your lawn needs. We hope you were more than satisfied with our performance. This season is coming to a close and this will be the last billing for the year. If you need any last minute services before winter sets in, feel free to contact us. We will be sending out a letter in March to welcome you back to the new season. Until then, we hope you and your family will have a safe and happy winter.

Sincerely,

Joe Smith
888-555-9487
Email: joe@gopherforum.com
Web: www.gopherforum.com

Snow plow and property maintenance letter.

If you are looking to provide snow plowing services or property management services to home owners in your area, here is a great sample letter you can send out in fall to line up potential customers. A lawn care business owner told me "I provide property care taking and snow removal service during the non lawn season. Here is a letter I sent out to over 200 homeowners. Most of the homeowners don't permanently live here, but have a second home here. Out of those 200 letters, I received 8 responses and ended up getting 4 snow plowing jobs, one property care taking job, and a lawn contract for next year."

Dear Homeowner,

Please allow me to introduce myself to you. My name is Joe, and I have lived in Your Town, since this Month of this Year. During much of that time I have operated my own property management company.

Winter in (Your Town, Your State) is just around the corner. One thing that comes with winter is snow. It is not a question of whether or not we will receive snow, but more a question of how much. With snow on the way, it is also a question as to who will keep your property cleared of that snow.

There is nothing like the falling of fresh snow. It seems to brighten up the world and give it a sense of freshness. It also means it is time to get to work and clean up the driveway and the sidewalks. It's not always an easy task and not always a task that one can accomplish for several reasons, such as health, time or your not being here to take care of it.

Snow in the driveway should never be ignored. It is important to have a clean, snow free driveway. A snow filled driveway is like having a sign on your home saying Vacancy.

Added security to your home can start with something as simple as plowing the driveway and this service can be added to our weekly property inspections.

Along with clearing snow, I provide weekly house checks and inspections for a number of homes in the area. Your home can be placed on our schedule to be checked each week for problems ranging from water leaks, broken windows, roof leaks and any other problems which may arise in your absence.

We offer a service to take care of your property when you are not here to do so. Among those services are things as simple as watering your house plants and starting your vehicle while checking your home.

We are fully insured and have a list of references which can be viewed on our website. You will see that we are dedicated to our job and our clients and treat every property as though it was our own.

Contact (Your Lawn Care Services) to take care of your property. We will gladly put you on a schedule to have your property cleared of snow and your unoccupied home checked each week.

Sincerely,
Your Name

Lawn care business customer referral letter sample.

If you are looking to increase your lawn care customer base, a great way to do it is by increasing your referrals. How do you increase your referrals? You can start by simply asking your current customers to help you out with a letter. You would be amazed at how your current customer base would be willing to help you out if they only knew you wanted them to do it. Here is a sample letter you can edit to fit your specific needs. One thing to keep in mind before you send out this letter is do not send it with an invoice. Your customers probably won't be in the mood to help you when they are writing a check. Instead, pick another time during the month to do this and include a few business cards in the letter.

Homeowner
1 Your Street
Your Town, State Zip

Dear Homeowner,

I would like to take a moment to thank you for helping us grow last year. We really appreciate you helping "spread the word" about our company and services we provide.

As we are entering the spring of this new year we would really appreciate your continued support. If you know of anyone, friends, family or neighbors, who are in need of the services we provide, please consider suggesting us. We have included a few business cards you can hand to them.

In return for your referral of any job totaling $100 or more to a new customer, we will provide you with any one choice of the following services: one cubic yard of double ground hardwood mulch, a turf fertilizer application, or one free mow.

Thank you again for your support of our company. We look forwards to seeing you this spring.

Should you require any new services this year, or if you have any questions, please do not hesitate to contact me.

Sincerely,

Your Contact Information

A landscaping and lawn care debt collection letter that works.

Do you have a customer or customers who tell you repeatedly the check is in the mail? Maybe they have even go so far as to tell you they aren't going to pay you. A lawn care business owner I was talking with had to deal with this issue until she sent out a letter that got her dead beat lawn care customer to pay up.

She wrote and said she was dealing with two deadbeat customer situations. This is how she dealt with them. "First, I called the Small Claims Court in my County and gathered information on starting a small court claim. I found out how much to file, how much for the Sheriff to serve papers, etc. Then, I gathered my information regarding my deadbeat client; like the dates we performed lawn & garden maintenance and filled in the blanks. I wrote a letter to the dead beat customer and in it I stressed she had 5 days after the receipt of the letter to settle her bill. If not, then I will file a claim against her for theft of services.

I went to the post office and sent the letter registered mail. Three days later, I received her payment in full. I ran to the bank and deposited the check hoping she didn't put a stop payment on it! Accompanying her check was a little nasty note stating that she was the one who fired us, but that doesn't excuse her nonpayment.

Here's the lawn care business debt collection letter format that I used. I removed the personal information so others who use it can just fill in the blanks appropriately."

Dear deadbeat:

You had hired ABC Lawn Care Company on (insert date) to perform garden maintenance at 3 week intervals, starting on this day. At the same time, you hired us for lawn maintenance at an agreed price of $$, starting this day. Since then, I've performed garden maintenance per our contract on this day and lawn maintenance was performed on the following dates. Payment terms per our contract are due upon completion. Payments for the services listed above are now due immediately. Despite several phone calls to you to collect payment, you have stated on 3 separate occasions that your payment is in the mail. Since I have not received payment to date, your services were terminated by ABC Lawn Care Company on said date, due to theft of services.

As per our contract, I am requesting to be paid $$$ for our services.

If I do not hear from you within 5 days from the receipt of this letter, then I will file a petition with small claims court in Your County.

I look forward to working with you toward a resolution of this matter.

Very truly,

Your Name

What to include in your hand written thank you card?

Each year you should consider dropping off a hand written thank you card to your lawn care customers. You don't have to do them all at once. Just break down your lawn care customer list and do them step by step. This is a great way to build up your lawn care business referrals.

What should you include in your hand written thank you card? How about something like this.

Dear Customer,

Thank you for your business. I really appreciate it. Keep in mind if you need to get in touch with me for any reason, please call. Also if you could, please pass on a few of my business cards to anyone you know who might need my services. I would be thankful for any referrals you could send my way.

> *Sincerely,*
> *Joe*

Don't forget to include three business cards along with the thank you card.

Lawn care business press release idea.

In general I don't think lawn care business owners utilize press releases as much as they should. The media, especially the local media, is always looking for a news story. Why not give them one? What does it cost to offer them a news idea? Nothing more than a little time to write up a press release and send it out to the local press.

Now I know that can be a little difficult and perhaps daunting of a challenge so I thought it would be a great experiment to put together a sample press release article idea that you could use and change the names in it and then send out to your local press. Then any lawn care business owner who used this idea and got an article written about them, could get onto the Gopher Forum and tell us about how it happened and their experience. Plus they could tell us what kind of results came from being spotlighted in the local media.

Title: Local resident offers his own economic stimulus plan.

With our economy in a downward spiral and the federal government offering up what seems to be a new economic recovery plan every week, local resident John Smith, has an answer on how to fix this mess we are in.

In one word, he summed up his plan. "Jobs. We need to create jobs." We can no longer rely on our current employer to protect us in an economic downturn. Businesses are going belly up all over the place. It's our duty to harness our energy and creativity and create jobs."

John Smith is the owner of Smith's Lawn Care which has operated in town for the past X years. "If we each take a moment and think about what our skill set is, we could create a business and create jobs, today! Right now! We shouldn't be looking to the government to hand us out an unemployment check. We need to create jobs and hand out a paycheck. We need to make our township, county, state and country the best it can be by creating.

Each one of us can do something another person needs. Can you babysit? Can you cook? Can you cut lawns? Can you paint a house? Can you build a website. Figure out what you can do and do it. Then hire someone to help."

With this Spring just around the corner, John plans on hiring local residents to help perform lawn care and landscaping services. "If we each do a little, together we can do a lot."

President John F. Kennedy's inaugural address concluded with this famous line. "And so, my fellow Americans, ask not what your country can do for you; ask what you can do for your country." Now more than ever we need to do for our country. We need to fix this economic situation. We have the power to fix this situation and we will fix it if each one of us stands up, takes a step forward and reaches out to others to help them.

Create jobs!

Now you can either send this to your local paper as a press release to get them to call you and interview you or you can send this in as a letter to the editor. Take the text, change it around to fit your specific situation and send it in! It's free advertising and it's a positive message that will reflect positively on you and your business.

Try it out and let me know how it works.

Promoting your lawn care business through local schools.

I am so impressed with the creative marketing ideas that come through the Gopher Lawn Care Business Forum. One of our friends shared with us his idea to market his lawn care business through local schools and teach kids some useful information along the way.

He posted a letter he is planning on sending to the local school principals and I am going to include it here along with my view on what else you could do.

He wrote "I'm emailing principals of schools in my area. I hope this works. This is a sample of the letter.

Dear Mr/Mrs _____ of _____ School

I am the owner of Joe's Lawn Service here in Your Town.

I came up with a fun & creative project that all students can take part in.

My plan would be to explain to the students about the complexities of starting their own business.
Example:

The Plan (is it possible? is it needed?)
The Budget (when can I start?)
The Requirements (what is needed)
Marketing (who/what/when/where/why)

Competition (how to lead, how to gain without lowering your service costs, etc)

After the above, I would ask of them to take a Joe's Lawn Service flyer & business card home with them.

If the household owners of the students are interested in hiring my lawn care service, each student will gain $20.00 for their support, & the homeroom class of the students will receive the required amount of Pizza.

I would encourage students to work hard & focus while in class, letting them know & to understand the importance of putting in the hard work while the opportunity is given to them. I would explain the possible outcome of people who have refused to take school seriously, & how they are currently struggling.

I would love to explain to the students the difference of having a job vs having a career, & the cost of living.

I believe most students don't know about the frightening truth of what their life will become once they are on their own, without someone to take care of them. I also believe once the students get an idea, it will give them a goal to achieve.

Thank you for your time,
Joe "

Now I thought this was a fantastic idea which you could take in many different ways. I am thinking you might get a better response if you don't make it too commercial. I love everything commercial, but with schools and kids, they may be a little picky on this. I would probably take out the section about the business flyer and the pizza.

Instead of saying that, you could do other things. Like maybe come up with a coloring book sheet that allowed the students to color in a mower or maybe an outline of what you talked about.

You could also hand out promotional magnets or tshirts or stuff kids would like. The magnets could promote mower safety and list 5 safety points and at the bottom it could have your business name and number. They could be handed out at the end of the seminar to let the kids hang their coloring page up on their refrigerator.

You could also talk about outdoor power equipment safety and give a hand out on the dangers of the equipment.

Create a coloring page you could hand out to the kids and get them into the activity of coloring in the page as well as writing what safety equipment should be worn while mowing a lawn.

Experiment with this topic and see what you can come up with. If you end up offering this seminar, make sure you take pictures and send them to your local newspaper to get even more publicity.

Are your lawn care customer letters personalized?

One of our Gopher Lawn Care Business Forum members put together this great letter to send out to his lawn care customers. When I asked him about the letter he said "a letter from me might just remind them that their lawn service is friendly & shares apart of itself with them.

I also promote a referral system that offers money. I think it is better because more people like MONEY than they do random items…

I'm hoping to remind people we have a referral system & that everyone can take part in!"

One of the things I like about your letter is that you included your picture in the letter. I haven't seen that done before. What made you decide to do that?

"The point of my letter is to bond with my customers, by giving my company a face.

I want them to know we are real, & not machines, numbers, or just a pretty logo. We are human just like them & I believe they will feel more comfortable with knowing that.

Looking official is great, but sometimes too official can be scary for customers. If I were to deal with a company, I'd like to get to know them before I hire them. It would make me feel safe & probably more trusting towards them.

A logo doesn't do a company full justice, the company needs a face."

These are all great things to think about when putting together your own lawn care business letter. Below is a letter sample.

Date

Dear Mr. Thomas Smith

All of us at Joe's Lawn Care would like you to know, hiring our service is greatly appreciated. We try our absolute best to accomplish the required tasks, which you have hired us for.

Our mission is to provide our customers with the best service possible, adding a touch of generosity to remind you that we are human and unlike other lawn care services, we are not out to drain your wallet.

As a new company, we are unfortunately limited & unable to expand gracefully. The competition is this business is growing. The only way Joe's Lawn Care is able to expand is to write out fair estimates and also gain customers with great consistency.

We look forwards to updating our snow removal equipment and giving everyone the chance to be able to afford snow removal services.

Joe's Lawn Care has big plans and we would like for you to take part on our journey. Our referral system has been changed, though you still have the choice to redeem the previous items.

Our new referral system.

If you refer Joe's Lawn Care to somebody and they hire us for the entire season, meaning all monthly payments have been received, the cost of your lawn service will decrease accordingly.

1 customer - $15 off
2 customers - $25 off
3 customers - $40 off
4 customers - $55 off
5 customers - $100 off

You have the option to pay even less with Joe's Lawn Care, though this is a limited time offer so you must act now. The more customers Joe's Lawn Care gains from your efforts, the less you will be paying!

Once again, thank you for your support.

Sincerely,
Joe Smith

Lawn care marketing in a cup.

If you are looking for a way to stand out when you do your lawn care estimates, why not do what one of our Gopher Forum members does when he visits a home to do a lawn care estimate.

He wrote "Every time I do an estimate, the estimate sheet, brochure and biz card go in a plastic cup. The cup I use is silk screened to display my logo and business contact information and placed on the door step. I feel most people won't throw it away, so the shelf life of the cup is worth it. You could do this with can coolies as well but they are almost 3 times the cost. I can get cups for about 50 cents a piece depending on the quantity."

How often when you do estimates is someone home? Do you hand the cup to a lot of people when they are home or are most out during the day and just want you to come by and leave an estimate?

What kind of response have you gotten in using the cup? Has it improved your estimate acceptance rate?

He responded "I do lot's of estimates, at least 100+ in the Spring time alone. Usually no one is home, so I leave the cup, estimate, brochure, etc. on the front porch. I can't say if it gets a better response or not, but I feel with the right materials it makes you look more professional and not like some fly by night company."

This is also a great way to promote your lawn care business by going door to door and leaving a flyer in the cup as well. Maybe even include a pen. So consider these ideas next time you are looking for a way to stand out.

Lawn care marketing direct mail response rates.

Most lawn care business owners experiment with direct mail for their lawn care marketing and often wonder what kind of response rate they should be seeing.

A Gopher Forum member sent out mailings for his lawn care business and asked this question.

He said "I've sent 475 color stump removal promotion flyers and I only received 1 estimate so far. I've seen most of my flyers in the garbage can at the post office. Does this mean people are tired of flyers?"

Another lawn care business owner responded by saying "No that is actually a reasonable response from 475 flyers.

A good industry standard for direct mail is a 1-2% response rate. But I'll tell you it's been a long time since I've seen a 1% response from any of my mailings. So at 1% you should have gotten about 4.75 calls. That might seem a little low...

However... You are marketing a service that is VERY unique. I don't know how it is in your area, but in mine, there just are not that many stumps that need to be ground down. For example if you did a flyer for "grass cutting" let's say, you know that just about everyone who sees your flyer, (or if you distribute them you can make sure) has a lawn. You don't know if everyone, who saw your flyer, has a stump that needs ground down. So you have shrunk your market. The same would be true if you marketed dog fence installation. If you mailed to every home in a neighborhood, you have no idea who has a dog or not. Even though your flyer has other services on it, the only thing that customers see is the "stump grinding" headline at the top.

Since customers only look at these things for a split second, they are not seeing anything else but the main selling point. If they are interested in that, they might look at your other services, but not unless they want the main service your offering on the flyer. Does that make sense?

So I say if you got one from 475 that is a good response rate. I think many people don't realize how many flyers, postcards, door hangers, or whatever… it really takes to really get a large number of sales.

Don't get frustrated, keep putting them out!!!"

Lawn care business flyer response rates.

Have you been handing out flyers, trying to promote your Spring lawn care business services and not getting the response you thought you would be getting? There could be many reasons why this happens. Could it be your headline? Or maybe even your offer? Let's look into this.

A lawn care business owner wrote us and said "I've put out approximately 1,500 flyers and have only had 1, maybe 2 calls. I'm offering a month free with an annual agreement and have put a list of all the things we do on the flyer. What is going on?"

A business owner replied "WOW!! A month free?!?!?! That's crazy that people aren't calling and two that you would offer that! LOL

Keep your head up the business will come!! I normally get 1% to 2% call backs on flyers. I think that's the norm. My only suggestion would be this…and it might sound crazy so hang in there with me.

If it seems that most people are only getting a 1% to 2% call back on flyers…maybe you should put out less flyers at a time BUT put them out more often. I started putting flyers out the middle of Jan and I went out 4 times (once each weekend). I put out between 200 and 300 fliers each time (about a large subdivision worth) but I got about 1 to 2 calls each time. All that said I got 9 customers from that, and I only put out around 1,000 fliers. I'm up to 13 customers so far the rest I got from referrals.

I am also participating in a women's conference here where I live.

It's a sold out event and there will be 300 people there and about 20 vendors. So I've been prepping for that. Since the majority of the guests will be women at the conference I had gift certificates printed good for one lawn service. I figured that would be a good gift to give their husbands. Father's day is coming up…or even themselves…a lot of servicemen from my area are deployed right now so that means no husband to cut the yard. I put the price of $45 on the flyer and will have one displayed at the table…that gives me a little wiggle room…just in case I may need to take 10% off."

Another business owner said "I'm distributing about 2,000 fliers a week. There are so many neighborhoods where I am at that even at the rate, I won't be able to get everyone in my coverage area. Interestingly enough, my only new business lately has come from a yard sign I placed at a busy off-ramp on a major highway coming out of my area. Maybe give that a shot too!

I hit each house once. It's just not physically possible to hit a house a second or third time with the amount of flyers I put out alone. Although, I've been thinking about hiring someone to also help me distribute them out. The only problem with that is all my flyers have different prices on them. I put them accordingly on houses which I would charge that specific amount."

A third member suggested "you can't just sit there at the phone waiting for people to call. I've got people that called me last summer to do a fall cleanup and they originally had my 1st flyer from when I started my business 3 years ago! They held onto the flyer for that long! Some people/customers actually take your flyer and think about it."

A fourth member shared "Here is your solution . . .

1. Stop advertising price, you could be scaring potential customers away that you could up sell to.

2. Multiple exposures are the only way to do direct mailing.

3. Example for number two - Husband gets my pressure washing flyer and says ah yes the house is dirty. The door bell rings, he gets distracted and he sits the flyer down. He comes back to the couch and looks for the ad? Oh well let's see whats on tv.

4. While at the door the wife comes through cleaning and in the trash your flyer goes BYE BYE

5. Next week he gets another flyer from me. "Oh that's the company I needed to clean my house *ring ring* "Thank you for calling ABC Power Washing and Lawn Care how can I make your life easier?"

6. The rest is history!!!!

MULTIPLE EXPOSURE IS THE ONLY WAY TO GO TRUST ME . . .. Find a nice little mailing list of local potential customer addresses. You can go door to door as well. Shoot for around 1k and mail the hell out of them.

PLEASE TAKE THIS ADVICE IT WORKS!!!!!

If you don't believe me do an internet search for 'direct mail marketing' and read some articles they will all say you need to do 4 -7 mailings to get full results."

Ultimately all these responses really seemed to help the lawn care business owner who asked the question and started this discussion. He said "thanks for the advice! I've been thinking for weeks now whether or not to include a price on my flyer. Generally, I post flyers out at night. I rarely ever get a good view of the backyard, so I just estimate or "guesstimate" in my case.

I created a new flyer with a free template that I found on The Gopher Forum. There are 2 on a page, so I get 150 printed out, which, when cut in half, gives me 300 flyers. The print place will cut them in half for an extra 2 bucks."

3,500 lawn care business postcards mailed and how many results?

Have you ever sent out quite a bit of lawn care marketing material and gotten back lack luster results or no results at all? It happens. What is really difficult about this is if you are just starting out and you spend a lot of money on marketing and then get nothing in return, you might feel like giving up. If this happens to your lawn care business, don't give up. Marketing is like fishing. You never know when it's going to catch you something. Let's take a look at a story from the Gopher Lawn Care Business Forum.

One of our members wrote "I wanted to send out postcards to promote my lawn care business and what I did first was ask my current clients in my area if they read ad mail? Their response was sometimes "if it catches my eye" and "if it is printed on professional cards." I asked about flyers and the majority said they do not read flyers. If printed on a color photocopy paper, it's used as kindling to start a fire. So the message to me was clear.

I hired a local marketing company, told them what I wanted, they came back with 3 designs. I went back to my clients and asked them to choose. I also asked people at the local market which one they liked. All but one selected the same card. I had 10,000 printed.

I then had it mailed into very specific areas of the city. It's a very rich area where for the most part, home owners hire someone to do all the property maintenance for them to keep up with the neighbors. 80% of my sales are attributed to this local area.

The message of this specific post card was to promote our organic products, professional lawn care and clean ups. The card is very sharp. I mailed 3,500 last Thursday, not one call or email has been generated.

Two weeks ago I ran a very simple short ad in a local newspaper, it cost me $18.50, it's drive was to promote our mini excavation service. I received over twenty grand in contracts and am still receiving calls all from that tiny ad.

So I guess there is a lesson to be learned. I am a bit shocked at no response at all. I know this area well and the card really should have sparked some attention.

I ask every caller or email, how did you hear about us, 97% is newspaper, 3% search engine. I am not including word of mouth. I also picked up three jobs from people who saw one of my trucks and wrote the number down.

So I will give it one more shot and send 5,000 into the upper middle class area and see what happens, it is a very expensive way to get the name out, even if I had one call.....

I was curious about why this happened so what I did this evening was to email a large number of clients asking if they received our lawn care card. Those in the area I sent it to did indeed get them, so I can now rule out the question of if they were delivered or not."

Another forum member shared his views on newspaper ads. He said "post cards and ad packs are usually intercepted by the wife who considers the lawn, the 'duty' of the man of the house and promptly discards it. I don't think postcards are worthwhile.

I also ran a block ad in our local paper in the services section. It cost me $120.00 a quarter (13 weeks). I started the ad last week (it comes out every Monday and is home delivered) and so far I have received 61 calls and my website is getting 35-40 hits a day. I wanted to get 50 new accounts this year and as of today I have gotten 41. I gave 11 estimates today and have 10 set for tomorrow.

I think newspaper ads make you look more 'real' to the customers."

Very fascinating information to consider when you are looking into marketing your lawn care business. What works in one area may not work in another but one thing is for sure. Paying more money on your lawn care marketing does not guarantee it will work better.

How one lawn care business owner is attracting more customers.

Sometimes the difference between success and failure can be so slight we just don't know when we are close to that line. Many times entrepreneurs can walk within inches of success but give up before crossing over. Recently one of the Gopher Lawn Care Business Forum members told us how he was having a great day. We are very lucky that he shared with us what he has been doing to improve the awareness of his lawn care business. Taking the small steps here and there as he has can potentially take your lawn care business onto a successful path.

He wrote "I had a great day, today!

I did 3 small lawns, gave 10 estimates and got 4 of them. When I got home, I had 10 phone calls to return and 11 emails replies for Free Estimates from my website.

A happy vent for a change."

That is fantastic news! What kinds of things have you been doing with your lawn care business marketing to see such a positive response?

"I added a blog to my lawn care business website to improve my search engine ranking. I now hold Google positions 1-5 for lawn care service in my area.

I am the only lawn care company that is licensed and insured in my area.

I made a deal with the local hardware store which has helped a lot. I buy my supplies from them (that they carry), rent my equipment when needed, and they display my lawn care flyers in their store.

When canvasing neighborhoods I leave a magnet ad. I either hand it to them or if no one's home I stick it on their metal door if they have one or on the doorknob it they don't. Flyers they just throw away, but the magnet goes on their refrigerator."

If you are looking to push your lawn care business forward, try some or all of these suggestions and you too might start finding yourself having great days as well!

$10 off lawn care customer coupon marketing idea.

What if, instead of lawn care business cards, you had coupons printed up that were the size of dollar bills. You could hold them in your wallet and when you handed them to people, they could keep it in their wallet as well.

You could hand these out to current customers to give to their friends or to people you just meet around town.

You could add in a few conditions like they can not be combined and maybe have an expiration date, but I think it would sure beat just getting a business card. This is something, as a potential customer, you could use!

Maybe you could make these coupons valued at $10 or even experiment with $20.

See how they work out. You could have your wife or husband give these out too. Maybe even your employees or your kids! Heck give your entire extended family some to hand out. Get everyone into the act of promoting your lawn care business.

One of our forum members wrote "I am going to try a few for pressure washing and offer a discount or free mowing service to build up my referrals."

Free mowing special offer. One week only, yard sign.

When you drive around town, I am sure you see plenty of Realty sign. Realtors can be quite creative in their marketing and we can learn a lot from them. What if you wanted to build out your lawn care route more and wanted to get more customers in the area where you have current customers. This would potentially make your routes tighter by having multiple customers living on the same block.

How can you do this? Well, what if you took a yard sign and added a "please take one" box on the side of it that said 'Free mowing offer. This week only.' You could put this sign in a customer's yard and leave it up for a week. Put a bunch of flyers in it that made a real enticing offer like 'spend quality time on the weekends with your family, not with your lawn mower. For one week only we are offering a buy one get one free trial of our lawn care service.'

If you call us today, we will perform one free lawn cutting when you buy one.

It's a great way to try us out and see how easy it is to take back your weekends. Remember this great offer is only available this week so call today.

I bet you will get neighbors walking or driving by to stop and see what this Free offer is.

Then the following week, put the sign at another customer's house and switch it to a different customer each week.

What would be great too is if you included a clause in your lawn care contract that would allow you to put a promotional sign in your customers lawn for 1 week a year.

A lawn care business owner wrote "in some neighborhoods it won't work, mostly because it's not allowed. I bet it could be extremely effective in some neighborhoods though. The sign and flyer box should be relatively cheap, so you really wouldn't be out much to at least test it.

For those neighborhood's that don't allow yard signs, I'd send every house on your customer's street a postcard after every service visit presenting the offer. It's not the same as the yard sign, and it costs a little bit more, but at least this way you're guaranteed to get your sales message delivered instead of depending on the prospect to pull the flyer out of the box!"

How to get lawn care & yard work on foreclosed homes.

With the economy slowing, more and more homes are being foreclosed upon. As they sit uninhabited, someone has to maintain them or they will fall into disrepair. Mowing foreclosed homes is easy work. There is no homeowner to complain about the job and it gives you a chance to make first contact with the new homeowner when they move in.

This is exactly what one of our friends from the Gopher Lawn Care Business Forum is doing. In fact, it's how he got his start in lawn care. He wrote "I'm just starting my lawn care service and to be honest I'm a little nervous. I got here by accident. After being a real estate agent for several years my business was killed with the housing crunch, so I went back to driving a truck. I drove a truck for most of my life. I also did network marketing and then was offered a business cleaning up bank owned homes. What I found was after you clean them up you get the lawn service. Normally they want two cuts a month for $100.00. I now have 17 homes, so I decided to expand it to regular homes."

I asked him, what advice do you have for lawn care business owners who are looking to get into the business of cleaning up bank owned homes? How can they get their start and are there any hints you learned or downsides to it?

He responded "I got into cleaning up bank owned homes by accident. I had a friend doing it and he needed some help just cleaning the house (I had a cleaning company 10 years ago). After I started cleaning some of his homes, I spoke to a real estate agent

I knew that was selling REO's (bank owned homes). She referred me to another company. When I called them, they asked if I could give them a bid to do everything, clean out the trash, clean the house and do an initial lawn cut.

My real estate friend gave me some average bid numbers for my area and included in all bids is lawn service. The companies that handle most properties are called preservation companies and most are nation wide. I haven't been getting too many bids lately I went from 2 to 3 a week to 1 every two weeks. The area where I live has a ton of people doing this kind of service. The preservation companies have web pages to fill out vendor applications.

Another good way is to look at the signs on bank owned homes and call the agent that has a lot of these properties and ask them if they are getting good service, they deal directly with the bank sometimes. There is competition in bidding. Bid too low and you don't make enough. Bid to high and you don't get the job. The worst thing about all this is I figure it will phase out over the next year but I could be wrong. This is why I'm trying to reach out to more regular homes."

Great advice if you are looking to expand into providing service on bank owned properties. Remember, once you get one property in a newer area, make sure you reach out to the neighbors with your door hangers and flyers to help expand your route. Maybe use a lawn sign in the front of the property as well. This one property could become your beachhead in your marketing attack to help you expand out farther and farther.

Marketing lessons we can learn from a Realtor turned lawn care business owner.

If there is one group of local business people I find that are constantly hammering me with direct mail marketing material, it's Realtors. They really seem to have their act together when it comes to promoting their name and face out to the local community. So lucky me and lucky us when a new Gopher Lawn Care Business Forum member joined up to say hi to everyone. He shared with us his story on how he got started with his lawn care business and some marketing secrets he learned as a Realtor.

He wrote "hello everyone, I just wanted to say hi and introduce myself. I used to be a Realtor. I learned a lot about marketing in real estate, but the most important thing is you can't beat a referral from a happy customer!!! When my wife and I started out in real estate we had no budget, so we made up a flyer's that we dropped off on door steps. We picked a good geographic area with 200 homes. We made the flyer with cool and interesting facts. We also included a recipe of the month and what the housing market was doing.

People loved it, but you have to know that you must hit a person 6 to 9 times to be noticed and you have to stand out. Fridge magnets are a great marketing tool. One of the best fridge magnets I have used is a fridge calender for clients, so your name is always on their mind. Constant contact is key, and follow up with this line:

OH BY THE WAY…
I'm never too busy for your referrals!!
Talk to you soon"

Great advice from someone who knows what works.

Co-market with a garden center to gain more lawn care business.

When you are looking to gain new landscaping or lawn care customers, consider reaching out to your local garden centers. Purchase your supplies from them and see if you can get a business card display at their registers. Then ask the staff who sell lawn and garden supplies to refer you lawn care business for any install projects.

One of the Gopher Forum members in the past had hooked up with a garden center and gave the store employees 10% cash on each job total, when they referred a customer to him to do a job with material that was purchased at the garden center.

Because of this, he had consistent business referrals all year round. He was always doing so much better than any other landscaping business around him. So the lesson he told me from that experience was cash referrals can make a huge difference in your bottom line.

I asked him, how did you work out payments to the employees who referred you business?

"Every week I simply stopped in at the garden center, if I wasn't already there buying supplies and I would just thank the person and pay them cash on the spot."

Another thing you can consider doing is some cross marketing with the Garden Center. You could hand out flyers with your ad on one side and the garden center ad on the other. You could do the same with the door hangers. Then you could either split the printing costs or have them pay the printing costs and you go door to door to distribute them.

You could even host classes on the weekends at the garden center on how to install certain landscape projects. If the customer finds doing the job themselves is too overwhelming, they can always call you to help them do or finish the job properly.

Team up with a real estate agent to promote your lawn care business.

Real estate agents are the first people to really make contact with new home owners in your area. The agent has already built up a bond with the new home owner and is in a great position to refer your services to them. Why not team up with one or many real estate agents in your area. Help them create a welcome to the neighborhood kit and give yourself a head start jump on your competitors.

One of our Gopher Forum members wrote us on how he got involved with a real estate agent to cross market his lawn care business to new home owners. He said "while I was working yesterday, a real estate agent stopped to talk to me. He has built a great referral program and a service package that he gives home buyers when they buy a house. He told me he wanted to put me on his "preferred" service providers list that goes in these packages.

Right away he gave me a coffee cup with his all his information on it and a Thanksgiving card and small candle for my wife. The candle had all of his information on it as well. What a great idea! He told me he would help me make a flyer like the one he gave me which was very professional and nice. Also he said he could help me grow my business, based off of referrals. I only talked to him for about 10 min because it was getting dark and I had to load up and leave.

On the front of the card there was a picture of a family around a Thanksgiving table that says "Happy Thanksgiving, thanks for making me a part of your life." On the inside is a recipe for pumpkin pie dip. It also includes his name and real estate office then "a referral is sending someone you care about to someone you trust. Thank you for trusting me." I think it's a great idea with the recipe and all. It also came in a bag with the candle.

I thought the card with the recipe inside and the candle with info was pretty cool. I'm going to do something like this with my Christmas cards. He seemed to be doing good with it."

I really like the idea. He positions himself to be the go to person in the community as he creates this network of contractors in the area with his referral group. This not only helps him build good will with the new home owner but he also builds awareness of his services through his contractor contacts. Both sides benefit.

The lawn care business owner then said "he called me last night and gave me a customer to contact for some work. I'm going to there house tomorrow for a bid. I was surprised. I have talked to a lot of agents and usually don't hear back from them. He said to let him know when I want to meet with him so he can help me make up some literature. He can probably give me some great ideas on a referral program since he's been so successful with his."

Does he want a referral fee for this? Or how does this work?

"No fee, he just expects the same in return. I run into people about twice an month that are selling their houses so I will refer him. He had a very good presentation for his service package and referral program. A notebook full of colorful, laminated pages that he has spent some time on. Not just something he threw together."

That is fantastic. You should contact other real estate agents to do this with and get a hold of more contractors as well to work together on welcome packages.

"Here is an update. I went out and gave the new home owner a bid and got a $650 job this weekend!"

This is a great example of how networking with others in your area can really help you reach out to more potential customers with minimal expense on your part. As we all know, keeping your expenses to a minimum is very important, especially when you are just starting out.

Marketing your lawn care business with only business cards?

Here in this economic slump we see daily discussions on the Gopher Lawn Care Business Forum about the difficulties lawn care business owners are having as they try to find new lawn care customers. One of our members had an opposing marketing view that is held by many and he is finding a lot of success now. Let's see how he is doing it.

He wrote "well these last few weeks I have been completely covered up with work. I have picked up several new yard accounts, plus 6 tree removal jobs at about $700 each (average). I have picked up 3 brush clearing jobs. One at $600, one at $1,900, and another at $4,250."

That is great news! Can you give us your advice on how you stay so busy? What should other lawn care business owners be doing or thinking about in order to get back on track? Especially if they recently got started?

He replied "well, most of my work comes from repeat business and referrals. Most of my new business comes from online classified ad sites. I have never spent any money on advertising, except business cards. I have a theory that once you start paying for advertising, you will need to keep paying to keep the work flow coming. So I've tried to avoid it from day one.

I would suggest just putting yourself out there and never turn down an opportunity to talk about work with someone. I have started up conversations with MANY people about what I do and the next thing I knew I was giving a bid to them, or someone they knew.

So I guess, talk, talk, talk, and put yourself out there. Let everyone know what you are doing, and don't be afraid to ask someone if they need something done."

What a fascinating insight! Now I would think not spending any money on advertising except for lawn care business cards would put him at a disadvantage, but it seems the opposite has happened. It is quite possible to make up for the lack of customers he would have to deal with by not paying for advertising, he has compensated for by being personable and working on his social networking skills. So I think this is a great lesson for us all. If you want to succeed and sell more, you need to talk more. Talk to anyone and everyone and let them know you can help solve their problems with your services.

Marketing your lawn care business outward from the center.

When the economy takes a down turn, there usually are many new opportunities for entrepreneurs to get started with their own business. A lot of times people will think about starting their own business but if they have a full time job, the job will most likely take priority over starting a business. But if you get laid off, you then can jump on the opportunity to finally start the business you wanted. Here is a great question and a great example of an entrepreneur taking advantage of his resources and his knowledge to get his new business off the ground. He wrote "hi I am totally new to all of this. I mowed lawns while I was younger and throughout high school in my neighborhood and can do just about anything there is. I was just recently laid off at an excavating business because people are not wanting to build new houses or buildings at the moment.

Right now as I am just starting it is frustrating trying to get new accounts. Beyond lawn care, I also am doing snow removal. I am not too good at this whole internet deal but I managed to start up my own website as well. I am trying to make a flyer right now with my plan to make around 1,000 flyers and just start going door to door. I do not know any other way to just get my name out there.

What are the best ways to go out there and get customers? Are there any suggestions out there to make my company look better than the others? I just want my company to stand out more than others so we look like we have been in business and so people would come to me more than other lawn care businesses

Thanks to everyone for the help!"

I think first off you should jump on promoting services you can offer right now, that can make you money now. If your new business doesn't start making money quickly, you may lose interest in it or others around you may push you to consider other alternatives. There is nothing like making a profit to show the nay sayers they were wrong and you are right.

So how do you do this? Get on our Gopher Forum and download some of the free winter snow plowing flyer templates. I have a bunch of them for snow plowing and holiday light decorations. Edit the flyers as you need to and start handing them out to family members and friends. Get business cards made up and hand them out to everyone you know. In fact, give them a couple each. Tell them you are just getting started and you would appreciate any work you can get.

Market to your inner social core first. That would be friends and family. Have them become spokespeople for your business and have them help get the word out about your business too by telling their friends, co-workers and community organization members. Hang up flyers where ever you can, such as in local stores. Go door to door and hand out flyers that promote your winter services. The more people you meet, the better your chances are of landing new customers.

You had also asked about standing out more than others.

First off you have to remember, people will prefer hiring someone they know over someone they don't. So if someone knows you, that is the best way to stand out. Second off, get yourself set up with a uniform. Figure out a color scheme you want to wear and get a shirt and khaki pants along with a hat to match. This will help you look professional and presentable. Then get signs for your truck and trailer. If you need a business logo, remember I have hundreds of free lawn care business logo templates you can download and use from the Gopher Forum. Always try and answer your phone during the day and always be friendly and approachable. This should help you win many people over.

Lastly if you have time, you should consider doing something that is both a good deed for your community and a publicity stunt of sorts to attract media attention. Since you will be offering snow plowing, why not consider starting a volunteer group that clears walkways and driveways of snow for elder members of your community.

Contact the local paper and tell them you are looking to form this group and you will be heading it. Have interested volunteers contact you at your business number or contact you through your website and ask for those senors in need of free service to contact you as well. Possibly offer it on a scale of the neediest first. This could be a great way to get your picture in the local paper and get the word out about your new snow plowing service. It will also build up goodwill within your community and free publicity. One simple article could really get your business launched.

So try these ideas out and let us know how they all work.

Lawn care flyers - should you include prices?

Should you include prices on your lawn care flyer or should you say free estimates and present the lawn care estimate in person? Let's look into question.

I was having a discussion on effective marketing practices with a bunch of lawn care business owners and there were quite a few viewpoints shared on this topic.

I asked the lawn care business owners if they included prices on their flyers and this is what they had to say.

One business owner said "when I go door to door to distribute my flyers, I put the price for that specific house on it, so if they don't like the price they don't call. It also has every thing they will get for the money ie. monthly, weekly, or bi-weekly mowing. I also include a coupon for landscaping."

What is your view as to why you put a price on your lawn care marketing flyer?

"Well I put my price on them because my area seems to have a lot of tire kickers. They want the cheapest lawn care guy so they'll call around and go with the lawn care business who gives them the number they are looking for. Also you get those one time lawn cuts calling because their family is coming and the grass is 3ft. tall.

I don't have time for games. In my lawn care flyer I show you this is what you get, this is your price as I view the front and my knowledge of the average back yard in the area. The mowing price can go up if the back has a lot of work or I have to use my 36″ mower. I've gotten a good or better than average response with my lawn care flyers.

I put out 1,000 lawn care flyers and ended up with 3 mowing clients. The problem is, when it's time to distribute the lawn care flyers it's also time to cut the lawns. That marketing window of opportunity will depend on where you live. Either early or late winter. I would say as soon as the grass gets some green to it people see it's a lot taller than they thought."

Another owner said "I think meeting the lawn care customer face to face helps you sell & I'd also like to think my clients aren't necessarily hiring me on price alone. I'm not the most expensive lawn guy in town but I certainly am not striving to be the cheapest, so a little salesmanship will come into play."

I guess on one side, you can say I put my prices on the flyer and the customer can take it or leave it and if they call they are basically saying I know your price and I am willing to pay that.

On the other side is the customer that calls for an estimate, you walk the property with them and give them a price and if they flinch or say no, you can play with the figures, within reason to try and land that job. That is where being there in person and the salesmanship factor is important. If you don't get the job then you wasted your time going over there and giving the estimate."

The thing I wonder is, ultimately can you command a higher fee by making the presentation in person, because isn't that what an estimate is? A sales presentation?

If you can command a higher price, does it make it worth your while over other estimates you may have went on but didn't get?

"It's worth it to me! You are not going to get every lawn care estimate.

1. You have to remember that you can't take the rejection personally when you are in sales.
2. If you're getting every single job you estimate, YOU ARE LOWBALLING and you are leaving a lot of money on the table.

To make a "sale" the customer has to buy the SALESPERSON, the PRODUCT, & the PRICE. If you're not there in PERSON presenting the full value of the PRODUCT then they are only buying the PRICE. You didn't 'make the sale', You are 'ON SALE!'

Take the time to meet your lawn care customers, yeah you'll waste time on some but you'll be more profitable & both you & the client will be happier doing business together. You may meet some people & see a personality problem right off the bat. If so you can decline to estimate or work for them (I've done that once) or price it high enough to where it's worthwhile even if they are a pain in the ass!"

The last opinion on this discussion was"I've always leaned on the side of giving prices only during final negotiation. It's hard to convey your work ethic which justifies your price without a face-to-face meeting.

Though there are lots of tire kickers, I've found equal numbers of people will wait until their lawn needs attention right away. Once they call, they are ready to make a deal. If you can demonstrate the skill set needed to make their lawns look great, you can often command higher prices at these final meetings.

On-the-other-hand, if your price is on your lawn care flyer you've already set a ceiling which is difficult to raise."

I do hope this insight helps you determine better if you want to include prices on your lawn care marketing material or not.

Does your lawn care business marketing have a call to action?

There are many ways to promote your lawn care business through various forms of marketing. When you are creating your marketing, do you include a call to action? If you don't, you might be wasting your money. I talked with a lawn care business owner who had at one point worked as an advertising manager and had quite a bit to say on the topic.

He wrote "despite what a lot of the 'never discount' people say, you really need one if you are going to advertise. I spent years as an advertising manager for a local media group (which included the largest newspaper in my area). When you find yourself debating on a "as low as $xx" statement, a discount, or something free. Free always gets the best response, but is also the most costly. Also free with a large stipulation (annual agreement) is not as good. I know this is redundant, but I learned a little about direct mail and it's always been about three things.

1. The right prospects. You can't sell lawn service to residents living in apartments or poor neighborhoods (maybe).

2. The right time. You have to hit them when it's relevant. The start of the season is a big time, but so is through the season, as unreliable lawn care business owners start screwing up.

3. The right offer. You have to give a call to action. Most folks will have already picked up a paper, phone book, or some other means if it was urgent.

If you don't do all three, it's just branding. Which is great for large companies that are looking for name brand recognition, but not folks searching for a measurable ROI (return on investment)."

These are some great lawn care business marketing tips to keep in mind the next time you are creating your marketing material.

A lawn care business sales secret.

When you are getting your lawn care business started and you don't have many personal contacts, the situation can be rough. Let's take a look at what a lawn care business owner did to go from getting no calls to getting many.

This business owner wrote and said "my flyers & business cards have been sent out all over, a lot of my cards need to be restocked in stores because they are almost all gone. Yet I have gotten no calls.

I only have a few days left, I can only do so much. I'm mass producing flyers again & plan to send them out to the other areas of my city.

I myself have walked door to door handing out 7,000 flyers & I'm losing it! I don't wanna be out for weeks distributing these flyers so I'm gonna just start a.s.a.p. without stopping until they are all out! Can someone tell me what the hell I'm doing wrong."

I responded to him by saying I think you are doing a fantastic job. What you are doing with your flyers and business cards is good, however, you will find more success selling people to people. Selling to those you know or those that know you.

Have you considered picking up the phone and try to sell to people who are existing customers or people you know?

Then what you can do next is work the neighbors of your customers. Tell them you are servicing Mr. Jones' lawn next door and you would like to service their's too.

He wrote back "alright, I decided to reach out to my snow removal customers from the previous year. They had all received my flyer, but they didn't know it was me offering lawn care service since I changed my business name. Once I talked to them and they knew it was me they insisted on hiring me.

I told them, the starting price for lawn service is $X.00, but because you are a snow plowing customer & you helped me out during winter, it will only be $X.00 – a discount.

You can't beat that price, but hey, they were also my winter customers so they already know me.

I now have tons of appointments next week…

I guess I learned something. Call people & SELL yourself!"

Remember this when you find yourself having a hard time getting your initial customer base. Call people you know.

Advertise your lawn care business on garbage cans.

A lot of areas won't let you put out a yard sign on your property to promote your lawn care business, but what if you put a sign on your garbage cans to promote your lawn care business? This could be a great way to build out your routes around current customers. Maybe keep the sign simple and to the point "LAWN CARE - 555-2192."

You could also possibly put signs on your customers' trash cans and give them something like a free annual aeration or something like that in return.

I never see ads on garbage cans and because of that, they might stand out.

Maybe you could allow each customer to use a can of yours that said yard waste on the cover and was used for yard waste? You could then take the can back when their lawn care contract ends.

The great thing about this is garbage cans will be on the street usually twice a week and people driving to work in the morning and coming home in the evening will see them.

To do this really cheaply you could create a stencil out of card board that you can use with a can of spray paint. Anything you can do to get the word out more about your lawn care business is a good thing, so keep thinking!

How to find lawn care clients when business is slow.

The lawn care and landscaping industry is a seasonal business. Each season brings about a change in the environment which effects what services you can or can't offer. In the Winter months, customers will also be looking to spend their money on holiday gifts. So with all this going on, how can you make sales with all these potentially working against you?

Here are some simple steps you can follow to drum up new work and sales.

- Go through your customer list and contact inactive customers. See if they need any end of the year yard or home handyman services to prep up their house for the holidays.

- Create a lawn care package special. For example, offer your current clients a discount if they re-sign up for lawn care service next year and pay you in advance. Maybe offer them a 5% or 10% prepay discount.

- Repackage your services or products to make them more attractive during the holiday season. What if you sold a gift package that included a toy snow plow truck with a gift card attached that said Free Snow Removal for the Winter. Or you could do something similar for lawn care service for the following year.

- Wouldn't that make a great gift for someone's relative? What if it weren't just a toy snow plow truck but a collectible keep sake Christmas ornament? It would be a great visualization of what service they would be receiving throughout the winter months.

- Experiment with new services. If you haven't offered holiday light decoration services why not consider that?

If you do decide to offer such gift cards, make sure you promote it. Send out flyers to your current customer base and hand them out in your community. Wouldn't such a present make a great gift? Maybe use the headline 'Show someone special you really care with free snow removal all winter long.'

Keep these ideas in mind when you are trying to drum up business in the slow season.

Marketing your lawn care business in an area with 14% unemployment.

A lot of areas around the country are dealing with high unemployment rates. When you are just getting your lawn care business started, you may find this adds to the difficulty of getting off the ground. A new business owner shared with me his frustrations. He wondered what he might do to stand out in a highly competitive environment.

"Hello all" he wrote "I live in Oregon and we currently have the 2nd highest unemployment rate in the nation (just a tad behind Michigan). In my county our unemployment rate is almost 14%. This is my first year looking to start my business part time. I've landed a few lawn care jobs, all by one have come from family or friends of family. All of my marketing has fallen flat.

Over 1,000 door hangers and only 1 call. Advertising in the paper, not a call yet. I am updating my online classifieds ad every 2 days, no calls. I'm starting to feel like my market is just too over saturated.

I have a normal 8-5 job and see at least 1 or 2 lawn care business owners on the road every day. Sometimes up to 5 or 6 (this is only a 7 mile drive). What's happening in your areas? I'm considering direct mail or search engine advertising as my next advertising campaign, but I am starting to feel like I am throwing my money away."

I replied to him that he could try and expand his marketing message or he could also experiment with the services he offers.

When you talk to your family and friends are they telling you what their view is on paying for lawn care at the moment? Are they cutting their own lawns more often?

Have you thought about offering other services that many homeowners can't or won't do themselves? Are there things your friends and family are saying they need help with?

He responded "most of them are cutting the lawn themselves. Even some who have over 6 figure incomes. Others have always had the same guys doing it. I don't want to lean on them to fire their current person just to hire me. That just doesn't feel right. A lot of the work I've been doing is non-mowing jobs. Like clearing a weed thatch, spraying herbicide, dropping some bark, replacing dead trees etc. I'm not sure what else I could offer, I'm sure you have some ideas?"

I think just making it known you are available is important. For instance, what if their sewer line backs up? Could they call you to snake out a line? You can rent snakes for $50 for half a day and charge a couple hundred to do the service. Most home owners aren't going to do that themselves. There are plenty of other services they won't do either.

This isn't about leaning on your friends or family to fire their current person. Everything is in a constant state of flux. New people move in. Old people move out. Their long time handy-man may move on to somewhere else. These things go on day in and day out. All you want to do is be that friendly face they know they can call to solve their problem.

Maybe a fridge magnet would keep you around until they were ready to call you.

I would keep letting them know you can help with all sorts of things. Changing a hard to reach light bulb. Cleaning out gutters. Fixing a roof leak. Trimming back a tree. Reseting a mailbox. Replacing a sidewalk?

I bet if you asked around, each person has a 'to do list' for their home, they never get to.

Maybe put together a lawn care business flyer asking potential customers what's on their 'to do list?' It might get people thinking about their long 'to do list.' Everyone has one and no one ever gets it done."

He responded "thanks, this has given me more to think about. While I had wanted to try and focus on my core business (mowing and maintenance) I might need to branch out a little to try and find clients."

What your core business is today may not be your core tomorrow. Experiment and see what works best for you in your area.

Lawn of the month marketing campaign.

Here is a lawn care marketing idea that you could use to attract new business with little investment.

What if you created a lawn of the month contest. Create a yard sign that says lawn of the month and each month pick a different lawn you service to become the lawn of the month. Stick the yard sign in the lawn and let it draw attention to the property and to your business contact information. Take a picture of the property and show off the property on your website. On your website, show the reader why you decided to choose this property as the Lawn of the Month.

Create a lawn of the month flyer. This flyer could say something like "We at Joe's Landscaping are pleased to announce the lawn of the month for October is Jim's lawn located at 123 Main St. When you have a moment, please drive by their property to view it. I hope this yard inspires you to create ideas on how your yard could look. Please give us a call and we will stop by to provide you with a free landscaping analysis. Our analysis will show you what we could do to improve your yard's aesthetics. Call us at 555-8372.

Hand these flyers out to homes in the area of the lawn of the month home.

You could even present the homeowner with a trophy or a certificate that you print out on your printer. Take a picture of you handing the homeowner the prize. This is a great way to maintain your great customer retention levels. If a customer feels appreciated, they are less likely to choose another lawn care service provider.

Send a press release to your local paper or home owner's association newsletter along with the photo and a little write up about your award and why you chose this property. You could also do this in conjunction with a local home owner's association.

Recession marketing ideas for your lawn care business.

A new lawn care business owner had a very unique marketing idea that had a political edge and wrote us about it. "Hello! I just joined the Gopher Forum and was looking to get opinions on a couple of truck magnets I designed for my boyfriend's lawn care business. I pretty much handle his marketing/advertising and recently noticed some local business putting out specials/adverts using the down economy angle. My boyfriend is currently interchangeably displaying one on the back of his tailgate above his website address and opposite his regular business magnet.

The concern is that he's a little worried the magnets may seem a little political/controversial. Personally, I think they will draw attention to the business/website because everyone can relate in this current economic climate and the text doesn't force an opinion per se (but I could be wrong).

I am aiming for potential conservative, liberal and indifferent customers appreciating the magnets in a (hopefully) neutral and humorous way. I want to increase the website traffic while being more noticed and seen as distinctly different amongst the current competition around town. He just started the business in May of last year after a layoff and is 30 accounts strong right now just by himself. We've baby stepped everything, pretty much in a methodical/grassroots/DIY level from the beginning."

I can totally understand his point but you know, to me that's what marketing is all about. It's all about being different. If it can be controversial, even better. You want people to be talking about your marketing and if it isn't different, if it doesn't stand out, then you aren't going to get attention.

One of the things that I have been amazed with is that it takes soooo much energy to get a business started and running, and you have to really be different from the average person to even attempt it. But why do the same people who are the adventurers, the crazy ones, those with enough energy to start a business then decide they have to keep things tame in their marketing? Why do they not want to stand out? What makes people so afraid to stand out? To be different? To gain attention? Especially when that attention can get you more work?

Take for instance, Richard Branson, owner of the Virgin empire, such as Virgin airways. Recently he was promoting his airline dressed in drag. He wore a cheerleader's uniform with a blond wig. Guess what, he got media attention and here we are talking about it.

If you don't do something different, you can only at best expect the same results everyone else gets.

So for all this, I applaud you for being creative!

"Thanks for your comments! Regarding the political marketing truck magnet angle, my boyfriend was uncomfortable with it on his truck and removed it about a week ago. I kept the picture of it on the website, however, but with the lead-in tag line above it that says:

DON'T COUNT ON BIG GOVERNMENT TO PROVIDE YOU WITH ECONOMIC STIMULUS,

SAVE MORE GREEN SO YOU CAN SPEND MORE GREEN

WITH JOE'S MOWING!

I think I will create a new magnet along those lines. Next time around, perhaps with dollars signs swirling about and/or superimposed in the background.

As far as the bail-out special we created and 10% off on prepays 3 or more months, more people have utilized the 10% off prepay promotion so far. Although we just recently created the bail-out special. I think by next month's billing cycle we will know if our monthly customers will be taking advantage of the discount. We don't advertise/push promotions yet to existing customers by emailing or snail-mailing them notifications. Although they are always encouraged to check the website for updated promotions and specials when they sign up and we note the Refer-A-Friend savings prominently on their invoices.

Right now we feel it's the customer's responsibility to check our website on their own. Our plan, sometime this year, is to send periodic postcards/emails to existing customers (quarterly or so) to remind them of updated/new specials and offer them (suggestive upsell) tips. We could do monthly tip, etc. emailing, but it would be annoying and spam-like in my opinion.

We currently have about 6-7 solid prepaid accounts. It was a bit hard to do prepays in the beginning due to it not generating regular cash flow. However, the couple of ones that we had in the beginning did help to fund some start-up equipment purchases. Once we established over 20 accounts (and we hit 35 officially this week!), prepays have been a nice chunk of change when the payments comes due. A prepayment on a new account today just helped us purchase a new backpack blower!

I am definitely all about interrupting the mind with different types of marketing a la Mr. Branson. I am actually thinking about investing in a fluorescent green bear mascot suit in time and holding a very prominent advertising sign for the business (with the website, of course) and dancing a VERY animated jig on the side of major roads just to see what kind of response it gets.

When my boyfriend goes out on an estimate call and meets with customers he often tells me about the positive feedback he gets regarding our door hangers and website, most especially. We offer a lot on our promotions on our specials page, all things we will honor in a heartbeat, but not as many people take advantage as you'd think (so we're not losing our butts per se). The general consensus seems to be, people do NOTICE our marketing attempts/specials and do respond positively without being prompted. My speculation is that they feel that they seem to be getting 'more' with our lawn service versus with the general competition and consider us a more value-added option, if only 'psychologically'.

Again, thank you so much for your comments! I love this website! I'll keep posting on successes and misses."

I followed up by asking her why not prompt your customers though?

For instance, why not come up with a special, say Spring flowers planted in your yard for $X9.95, but hurry and contact us by XX/XX/XX date. We need to get your order into our supplier to be able to offer you that discounted price.

Then a week before the date, send one last reminder email maybe upping the ante. Offer some additional option if they call you by that date.

The world goes by pretty fast and I like getting updates on sales when it's something I am interested in. I think others do as well. Don't you?

"I like and can see your point about using more direct and active 'prompting' with the way you presented that Spring flower special example. I just may try something like that and perhaps show a sample before and after picture pre/post-flowers, tree trimming or mulching via email or postcard to add a nice visual. Thanks for opening me up to the possibilities!

Delivering more than a customer will normally expect and providing a great first impression is what I am all about. Be it on site, online, in advertising or on the phone, etc. it translates to more bang and service for the buck, which they definitely get in reality."

So keep all this in mind when you are experimenting with your lawn care business marketing. Don't rely on the customer to seek out what your specials are. It's up to you to tell them. This is all a part of selling.

Lawn flyer distribution tips.

When you distribute lawn care flyers, how do you do it? Do you have any specific method you use? Have you found one way works better than another. Well here is a suggestion from one of our forum members that might help expand the way you think about this topic. He wrote "I just recently came up with a couple different forms I'm planning on using. These aren't my primary flyers however as I am experimenting with them. One is to stir up new business this year and the other is a pre-printed estimate sheet that's on a heavy weight pre-folded paper."

Very creative! How will you be distributing them?

"I was planning on targeting very large developments and just going door to door either leaving them on the mailboxes, or on the front door. The sheet that has the section for mulch is my "estimate sheet." That's the form I use when I receive a customer call to come to their property and give them a quote. One problem I am running into is after I give the quote, how would you suggest following up on it?"

That's a good question. Do you try to seal the deal on the spot when you give your estimate or how do you go about giving your estimates? Do you leave them in a mailbox? Is the customer present?

"Most of the time when I am giving estimates no one is home, they are usually working. By the customer's request I either leave the estimate in the door or in their mailbox. I think handing the customer my estimate face to face would be ALOT easier to close the deal and get a contract signed right then and there but its not a perfect world so what do I do for the customers that I am forced to leave the estimates for them to review???"

Another business owner suggested "it is always better to give your estimates while you are standing with the customer. It's more likely then, that they will give you the go-ahead. The exception to this is if it is a large job and you need to go home and run the figures and do some calculations. Even then you should present it to them in person after your figuring is done.

Another thing is after you present the quote, and they want to look it over, wait 3 days then call them and ask them what they thought of the estimate. If they have reservations, ask them what the issue is and see if it is something that you can be flexible on and maybe meet them in the middle somehow. Follow these simple rules and I promise you will land more bids!"

I agree. I think if you try experimenting with this, you are going to see a big difference. You can also judge the persons reaction to the price when you are there with them. If the price seems to be a sticking point, you can always ask them what you need to do to get their approval so you can start today. Maybe you could give them a certain % discount on the spot to get the job.

Being with the customer allows you to feel out the situation.

"In person is best. It is easy for folks to say no, or just flat out disregard you, when you are not there. Like someone else said, if you are present you can feel out the situation and perhaps make some changes to seal the deal. You may have to sell why you are worth this money when your competitor charges $10 a week less.

If you are having problems being able to meet in person, you may want to play on the angle of liking to make in person contact so they know who they are potentially dealing with and who will be coming on their property to mow while they are not home. When you make contact, find something you have in common with them, but don't get too overly personal with them if this is the first time you meet."

I hope these ideas help you land more lawn care accounts.

Lawn care business flyer door to door distribution advice.

For every lawn care business start up that exists today, there is a theory on how best to distribute lawn care flyers, door to door. Everyone seems to have their own way to do it. Everyone thinks their way is the best way. Some put flyers in the door without knocking. Some put flyers in the mailbox. Some knock on the doors first. But which one of these will give you the best return on your efforts and money? I asked a group of lawn care business owners and here is what they had to say on the topic.

One said "I remember exactly how it was when I was first starting up my lawn care business. I would spend-spend-spend and then wonder why I wasn't getting slammed with new customers! Flyers ARE great, but what's better is FACE TO FACE time with a customer and a professional image! I would recommend creating a 'script' of sorts and practice in front of a mirror so that your delivery is smooth and not forced. Get your opening lines down for when you first greet a "P.C." (potential customer) and most importantly BE YOURSELF.

After sending out 1,000's of lawn care flyers myself, I decided to invest in a 'uniform' shirt. It was just a pocket t-shirt, but it had my logo and I also got some hats. I would typically wear khaki or green work shorts and work boots too. And when the weather is cooler, khaki or green work pants. Blue jeans (and certainly not "cut-offs") were not part of my uniform. I just think it made me look 'unprofessional.'

Once I started actually knocking on the doors and TALKING to people, as I would gain their confidence and hopefully their business, I would then hand them a flyer, a fridge magnet and then…CLOSE THE DEAL. 'Would you like me to get started on this right away? I could begin by…..' You have to ASK for the order! Once you have them to this point, you know your time, your money, your effort, was all spent much more wisely than throwing darts blindfolded at balloons."

Another business owner added "here is the best thing to do from my experience.

Collect flyers from other lawn care companies one year before you start & months before the start date of your first year. Look at the pros & cons, & get to work on creating your own lawn care flyer!

Distributing lawn care business flyers can get very expensive and it costs me valuable time. I also have to rely on many people, & when they decide to work making flyers, is when I'm out of time & have to rush.

I had an extra 1,000 lawn care flyers created Tuesday night. I took the day off to think & relax… Wednesday, I went & handed out 1,000 flyers by myself, & tomorrow is my last day before May. I still have to bust my *** to make this work. It never ends, not until your getting paid.

You will never be done advertising even after you've been door-to-door to every possible house in several cities. I started off with 500 flyers, nothing happened. 12,000 flyers later I'm still preparing to mass print more. I might put together a team of 6 to hand them out for me at $10/hr, if I save on supplies I can spend on workers at least this one time.

You have to advertise when other companies do, & keep up with them. Most of them do the same homes 3 times! So your mission is to do so as well. Others may also use direct marketing so they don't have to bust their *** handing out flyers, but the cost to do this is ridiculous.

When to hand out flyers.

1st time: Before lawn service is needed, this reminds customers it's almost time, they usually toss it in the trash.
I got 4 calls per 100 flyers.

2nd time: Customers are taking the time to see what you offer compared to other services, it's still too early for them to give a damn. They will consider it when the time comes. In the garbage again!
This time I got 7 calls per 100 flyers.

3rd time: It's late, but the grass is looking good. Customers might have thrown out your competitions flyers & now have only you as their savior & last minute option. At this point lawn service is serious & needed.
I got 20 calls.

4th time: Yet to be fully discovered by me, but I believe if you can do it, you should!"

Keep all these thoughts in mind when you go out there marketing your lawn care business. Sometimes all you need to do is change one little element in your marketing strategy to really find success.

Positive press is good for your lawn care business.

Positive press can have a tremendous influence on how the public perceives you and your business. When people in your community hold you in high regard, they will want to hire you or purchase products from you. They will also pay a premium to do business with you because of the high level of goodwill you have within your community.

How can you get positive press?

I have two stories for you. The first involves an elderly woman who lived alone and lost her home to a fire. In the local paper, on the front page was this sad story of how a local senior citizen lost her home to a fire. It included a picture with smoke billowing from the old house. When the reporter asked her how she felt about all she had been through, the woman said what she was most upset about was that she lost her wedding ring in the fire.

The next day, a local jeweler was reading the article and he jumped on the opportunity to help out. He contacted the paper and said he wanted to help make things right by offering this woman a new ring he would create and present her for free. WOW did this make the news and this jeweler looked like a superstar. With a front page article on him the next week presenting the woman with a new wedding ring, he could not have paid to get such great attention.

Another great story was told to us on the Gopher Lawn Care Business Forum by a member. In his post he said "When my father was a lawn care business owner he saw a news show on another lawn care company company who screwed a 90 year old lady out of a job she paid them to do. They took a 50% deposit & never landscaped her house. It was on all over the news. My father thought this was awful & that it spoke badly of all landscapers in the eyes of the public. He contacted the old lady, met with her & arranged to do the job for her for free. He was going to pay for all the materials out of his pocket & install them. He didn't intend on getting media attention but the old lady called the news station back & told them how this nice man was going to complete the job for her for free.

They ran another piece on the local evening news, with that several nurseries contacted the news station & offered to supply the materials for free. The press did another story & interviewed my father while he was on the job & took a few shots of it after completion. My father got calls from people impressed with his generosity & wanting him to work for them for YEARS!"

So think about this the next time you see something that you feel isn't right and you can make a difference.

Make a section on your lawn care business website and include all the press you have received and make it a mission to do good deeds. Collect news on you and share it with visitors who come to your site. Use it in your other marketing material as well.

Easter promotion ideas for your lawn care business.

As business owners, we can take each holiday and use it to promote good will within our community and promote our lawn care business. All we need to do is add a touch of creativity and from where there was nothing, a new promotional idea can sprout. Such an idea can help you reach out and promote your lawn care business to your target market.

One of the things you could do is host a local Easter Egg Hunt in your neighborhood. You could have it at your store front, or on your property or at a local park.

Get a bunch of plastic Easter eggs and fill them with treats. Then hide them in different locations and let the kids run out and find them. They can be hidden in the open or out of site. Give each child that partakes, a bag or a basket to hold their eggs.

Maybe have special gift baskets for the first X amount of children that attend.

You could also dress up as the Easter Bunny and have pictures taken of you in a costume with the child sitting on your lap. Post these pictures on your website and have them available for download in their full size, by the child's family. This would be a great way to show off your community involvement and attract people to your site. On your site you could offer a holiday special package if the customer signed up by a specific date.

To promote this, you could send out messages through your online social network site. Or you could put the information on a flyer / door hanger. Have one side promote your event and maybe the other promote your lawn care business with your holiday special package available for a limited time. Make a post on an internet classified ad site about this. Depending on the size of the event, put an advertisement in your local paper. Create lawn signs to promote the event. Send out emails to your current customers. Send out postcards. Send out a press release before and after the event to your local paper with pictures of it.

This would be a great way to create a fun event that will draw in your potential customers and give you a chance to really stand out from your competitors.

Can you imagine if you do this for a bunch of years how it could really grow and kids will come back to you years later to tell you how much fun they had, thanks to you.

Try this out and let me know how it goes.

Fall leaf clean up marketing idea with inflatable Halloween decorations.

Halloween is a great time to put out yard decorations. There area many new items on the market to add some seasonal flair to your property. Some of them are inflatable and are lit from within for decoration at night.

Something you could do to promote your fall leaf clean up service is to use one of these inflatable Halloween decorations on your property and using a stencil, spray the message "Fall Clean Up 555-3029." It could be a great way to attract the attention of those walking by or driving by your home at night. You could also do this if you have a commercial location for your lawn care business.

You could even take this idea one step further and put up an inflatable Halloween display at the homes of your family or friends in town too to help promote your services further. Can you imagine how much attention you could get if you placed this at a busy intersection?

While you are at it, have you considered renting out such Halloween outdoor decorations to lawn care customers and providing seasonal home decoration as a service? It could be another way to make money in your slow season.

If you are out in your area raking up leaves and want to promote the service further to neighbors in the area, why not try this. Get some pumpkin leaf bags and on the blank side on the back, use a stencil to spray in your lawn care business phone number and maybe the words leaf cleanup. Place the bag where it will be easily seen by others passing by. Use one of these bags per job. That will really make it stand out and attract attention.

- Step 1. Get a bunch of orange pumpkin style leaf bags.
- Step 2. Create a stencil with leaf cleanup and your phone number.
- Step 3. Spray it on the bag with black paint and you got a great way to advertise.
- Step 4. Use one of these bags per job when you are bagging leafs to get the word out about your business.

Pumpkin & lawn care business card marketing.

I am always keeping my eye out for new and creative marketing ideas that can be applied to the lawn care business and I saw one that I thought was great.

Realtors who want to make money know they need to keep their name out, especially when people are looking to sell their homes. They also want to gain referrals of friends or family members through their marketing base. So the other day, there was this Realtor driving around with her SUV with the rear section of her truck full of these small pumpkins. She wasn't just stopping at every home on the street but instead stopping at the homes that were well kept and looked like they were worth something. Then she would get out of her vehicle and walk up to the stairs and place a pumpkin on their door step and leave.

I thought this was a fantastic idea. You could do this too. Why not get a bunch of pumpkins and tie some business cards to them. You could go out around town and distribute these pumpkins the way this Realtor was doing it or you could distribute them to the neighbors of your current customers using the clover leaf marketing technique. This could really help you stand out and add more customers to your current route. The more customers you have closer together, the more profits you will make due to the fact you will be traveling less between customers.

Maybe on the back side of the business card you could also offer a fall leaf clean up special! Play with this idea and you might find something that will work great for you.

Snow plow marketing idea.

Coming up with new and innovative ways to stand out with your marketing can be really tough to do. So if something works for others, why not experiment with the idea on your own. This marketing idea is sure to make you a favorite amongst your customers and neighbors. To promote your snow plowing services why not try this.

One of our forum members wrote us and said "here is an example of some decals/stickers I made for my snow plow clients. I wanted to give out buckets of ice melt to my snow plow customers but wanted my name and company info on them. You can get any sized bucket you'd like and slap a sticker on the side that includes your logo. Above your logo you could have it say complimentary ice melt provided by. And on the bottom have it say, please call for refills. I also made "Please keep covered" and "Use Gloves" stickers for the lids.

The great thing about this is you can re-use the buckets every year. You can fill the buckets with salt, ice melt, etc."

This is just fantastic. There are many things you could do with this. You could buy a bulk amount of buckets and get these stickers printed up, then fill each one. Stop by the homes in your area and drop them off on the front stairs possibly along with a door hanger explaining who you are and that you left this free gift. If the customer would need Winter snow plowing services, they could contact you and also don't forget to promote your lawn care services as well, for the Spring. The cover of the bucket or the side could have a sticker that say something to the effect of when it snows contact Joe's Snow Removal.

You could also include a coupon to help give the homeowner an additional incentive to call you within a certain time frame.

Now if you wanted to give these to only your paying customers as a thank you for signing up, you could go with a larger bucket but if you wanted to use them as a marketing tool and distribute them more widely, you could go with a smaller size.

A business owner who used the bucket idea wrote to say "the salt buckets worked extremely well!"

Thanks for keeping us posted on how using them worked out!

Performing acts of kindness with your lawn care company.

How often have you found yourself in a situation where you could perform an act of kindness to your lawn care customer or to a local member of your community? Have you jumped on these opportunities to really shine or were you simply in too much of a rush to get on to your next lawn care customer? Well it seems jumping on these opportunities to help others is not only good for those you help but for you and your lawn care company as well. Let me share with you some insights other lawn care business owners have experienced.

One said "here are a few words of advice that have worked well for me.

> 1. Do not grow too fast.
> 2. Find a niche and stick with it. Ours has been to not grow very big, we emphasize that an owner is on the property every week.
> 3. GIVE AWAY STUFF. I tell my guys that EVERY week we will do someone's yard for free, weather it is an old lady that is struggling, or someone that just seems too busy. This always comes back to pay off."

I asked him how he goes about finding who's yard to do for free? Also do you promote this? How do you suggest letting everyone know you do such good deeds?

"We do NOT promote this in any way. We don't even talk about it normally. Basically just being observant. If we see a little old lady sweating her butt off trying to mow her lawn in August, we just pull up and do it. We don't even worry about telling people we did it. We just think it is the right thing to do. That ladies' family will definitely know about it. Of course we give her a couple business cards before we go.

Another thing we do is try to get to know all our neighbors. What they do for a living. When we know these things, we can keep on eye on their lawns. If the lawn gets out of hand, we just take care of it. They normally know who it is."

That is wonderful of you to do that! Very kind!

Have you ever gotten any feedback from anyone later on where this act of kindness on your part came up? Or where you got a job because of something nice you did?

"Honestly, we pick up a job from it, I would say about 40 % of the time. Usually from another family member, friend, or neighbor. Do nice things and people talk. I would much rather have them talk about something positive that we have done."

Another lawn care business owner said "no doubt. I have also. Being honest and sincere will always pay off in the end. This is something we have also done in the past. I do not do it to promote anything or look to gain from it. I have done it because I have a kind heart.

One example is that I have an elderly lady that I mow for. Both her husband and her daughter were murdered, both years apart. So she lives alone. I have went up there, mowed her yard, sometimes on her birthday and sometimes on Mother's Day, and like always before, she'll walk out there with her check book to pay me and I'll tell her this one is on the house followed by happy mothers day or happy birthday. 'She'll say, I am going to whip you.' I'll say, 'you have to catch me first, lol.' This is something, without her telling me, that I know she appreciates, no doubt. She also on occasion puts an extra $5 or $10 in my check. I just save it up a few times and mow her yard again for free.

I have made true friends with all of my customers. We have a huge trust with each other. How many customers will walk out and give you a blank check and say, fill it out for what I owe you?? Or how many lawn care customers do you know that will give you a key to there house?? I have many!

I think it is great to give back to people, they will in turn give back to you!"

What great insight! It really gives you something to think about when you are looking to build goodwill within your community and grow your lawn care business.

Offering animal trapping services to your lawn care customers?

Have you ever considered offering animal trapping services? This is a great topic that was brought to my attention by a lawn care business owner. When you are offering your customers property maintenance, this is a service that could fit right in as an upsell. It could also open more doors to other potential customers who have yet to hire you for lawn care.

Think about this for a moment. What if a home owner is having a problem on their property with certain wild animals? Maybe you could set a small trap and catch the animal and then release it somewhere away from the home. This might be another easy service you could offer with very little additional overhead.

A lawn care business owner wrote "I have never thought of offering the service myself. However I do subcontract a lot of trapping / pest control work out."

That is a good idea too! For others looking to do this, would you suggest getting a referral fee for each one you subcontract out or should you just do it in return for getting referrals from them?

"I go with a 28% subcontract fee. I bill the lawn care customer and pay the sub-contractor. I add 28% on top of the sub-contractor's invoice. It goes that way for all my subs."

Do you find that the subs offer a discount or do they give you their regular price? Maybe the customer doesn't really care because they are happy with you.

"Unless I am giving them tons of service, they just charge me accordingly, like they would anyone else. I have never had a customer complain and I am very upfront if I need to sub-contract the service out. It saves them time and they understand that it takes my time to set it all up, collect money, pay subs, etc.

I have a very close circle of contractors I work with and I don't leave that circle unless it is an emergency. And yes, one hand washes the other."

When the storm hits, will you be prepared to profit?

When storms come through your area, are you prepared to service your community? Will you be able to remove fallen trees? Board up broken windows? Cover damaged roofs with large tarps? Pump water out of basements? Offer general property clean ups? I had a great discussion on this topic I want to share with you.

A lawn care business owner wrote "Well it looks like we will be hit with a hurricane on Sunday afternoon. Although things can change, I have been following this storm since it started and none of the computer models have changed their projected path.

It's projected to only be a category 1 when it hits here. The issue is a category 2-3 had hit here in years past and did massive damage to the area woodlands. I alone lost almost 300 trees, many of which still need to be cleaned up. In fact 90% of our tree work this summer was from that storm. It weakened millions of trees that seem to fall late in the summer when we start receiving the tropical storms that blow up the Atlantic.

Today was a 12 hour workday here but I still managed to get 50 gallons of gas and 30 gallons of diesel. I received 32 emails today some from current clients some people I have never heard of asking if they can be put on a list for tree clean up should the storm hit us as projected. In a sense I am not looking forward to this but at the same time it is a challenge that we are ready for. All three of my wood chippers and seven chain saws are ready to go. I picked up 10 x 24's of bottled water and lots of dry food to keep us going.

The only thing we will be short of is staff."

Would it be worthwhile to send out an email to your clients on how to prepare for the storm and if they have any tree problems, to call you?

"If I had the staff I would write a nice letter and email clients but if the storm is half as bad as they say this morning, we will be clearing and chipping for weeks."

Another owner shared "We had a tornado hit us yesterday…just down the road from me…very very close to home.

Generally what happens here is anyone with a truck and saw places a sign on the side of their truck with their rate and cell number. The local outdoor power center told me they sold over 300 saws in the past 48 hours. I now have over 60 requests to be placed on standby. I was out all day working with the crews removing trees near power lines, we use the excavators and tractors to put pressure on the trees and make them fall where we want. It's really good danger pay for doing this work, we charge $125.00 per tree, that is just to fall it. Then if they want we will send in a crew to cut it up and chip. I have two 8″ tow chippers which frees up the tractors for other work, I rented two trucks this morning and everyone headed out."

Most asked for pressure washing jobs?

If you are looking to add pressure washing to the list of services your lawn care business offers, you might be interested in knowing which pressure washing jobs are most commonly needed. This was brought up in a discussion on the Gopher Lawn Care Business Forum.

One lawn care business owner asked "I wanted to get into pressure washing. How do you go about it? I'd like to do sidings, driveways, outdoor furniture, maybe even windows. What product do you use with your pressure washer, or do you just spray water? I couldn't imagine it being a tough job and it sounds fun!

What kind of problems can you run into? Creating small floods & soggy grass? How do you charge? etc… I guess I'll offer this service starting Monday! I got two pressure washers waiting for work."

Another responded "pressure washing has been a small gold mine for me. There just are not many companies here offering the service and with vinyl siding and so many trees, dirt, grime, mold etc are an issue pretty much everywhere we go.

How I got into it was to advertise the service, response was amazing so I bought the equipment, then added a 2nd and 3rd unit when we were running 5 business days behind.

We use a mixture of Simple Green when we spray. I buy it from a local big box retailer, they have 5 products depending on what you are doing, works amazing.

We charge by the job, there is no generic way to calculate but I average around $65 an hour. A 10 X 16 ft deck with say 10 stairs and a railing will generally run $225 and take the guys about 2 1/2 to 3 hours. Siding is the choice and the fastest job. A single story home say 34 X 26 ft will run $400.00 and take about 4 to 5 hours.

Do an internet search and buy what is called a turbo tip. These things will remove anything. They have a quick connect much like an air line has. We use them for really tough jobs.

A 2,500 psi power washer will be a little slower but will do an excellent job on siding and most decks. I don't think it will remove paint. We have to use 5,000 psi for that and the white tip.....the paint just flies off then.

Residential pressure washers, those that are rated 1,500 PSI are a waste of time. We pick up a lot of business from people that have spent a day trying to clean with one then calling us. We have two power washing units. One is 3,400 psi and the other that is 5,000 psi. Each are gas powered and require 4 gpm.

We don't get many driveways. The #1 request is for siding followed by decks. The 5,000 psi unit will remove paint from siding using the proper attachment. We charge $125 an hour for that service, we get a few jobs. Good luck, it's excellent money."

The importance of vinyl signs on your landscape trailer.

Are you using your lawn care truck or landscaping trailer to attract attention? Sure your vehicle and trailer need to be functional first but it's quite amazing how this simple step can really change the image of your lawn care business and bring you more customers. Getting vinyl signs and lettering on your truck and trailer creates the feel of your business being solid, dependable and here for the long haul.

One of our friends on the Gopher Lawn Care Business Forum shared with us his experience of going through the process of getting his vehicle lettered and what it has done to improve his business.

He wrote "I finally have one of my landscape trailers done with vinyl lettering. I did all the wording. A local sign company did suggest a few words be removed and I agreed, they also chose the colors. The lettering is green and has a white border/shadow, when the sun hits it, it looks really cool. The owner of the sign shop and is also a lawn care client of mine. She does real nice work. She changed what I wanted to do to the truck saying I should keep it simple, not too many words, just get the prospects attention.

At first I had listed too many services we offer. Snow removal, aeration, driveway grading, trenching etc. She said, people are either going to call or more than likely go to your website, list your services there. All you want to do it catch the prospects attention and go from there."

How important do you feel it is to have signs on your truck and trailer and have everything looking top-notch versus simply being functional?

"This really depends on the target client one is going after based on the feedback I have received. Our company is after the upper middle class, high class customer, granted we will do work for just about anyone though.

In a round about way I asked maybe 15 clients about vehicles, do you judge the potential service provider by what they drive, what they wear, tools they use etc. The feedback was as I suspected, the vehicle and dress reflect to them how well the company is doing. They said a company that has a good looking setup to them will do good work and that is the company they will hire.

I suspect to some degree it's an ego thing, they do not want a rough looking service vehicle/trailer etc parked in front of their home doing work on their property.

Personally I know this thought is not correct. Through the years, I have taken many things to 'hole in the wall operations' for repair and it was the best repair going. An old fellow, years ago, used to tune up my mower and chain saw every Spring. It was a very sad looking operation, he was about 70 at the time and had been doing this all his life, his work was unmatched. There is a welding operation about 10 min from my house, same deal, the place is a disaster however their prices are great and their work excellent.

It's a tough call as one has to get their name out there and vehicle/trailer lettering is critical. I also hear very often from doing estimates 'You must be a real company as you do not have magnetic signs.' Actually I do at home for when I first started however I had never thought people would be so critical of them. There are so many fly by night lawn care service guys out there, people seem to be very careful when hiring a new company and these are issues people consider. Whether they tell you or not."

Lawn care business uniforms.

One simple way to easily make your lawn care business stand out from others is to wear a uniform. The more outrageous the colors, the more attention you will attract. But in general, most small lawn care businesses don't wear lawn care uniforms. So the simple act of wearing one will make you stand out.

One of the members of the Gopher Lawn Care Business Forum shared with us his insight on wearing a uniform. He wrote "I know that all of you want to look your best when you are out there on the job site and have a professional look for yourself and staff, so I have a suggestion for all.

If you don't have a big budget for purchasing these items for yourself or your staff, here's an idea. I came across this when our linen company representative came by last week. I ask him if his company had any used outfits for sale that are in good condition. He said that his company has a wide variety of them for my choosing. He told me to name a color and style and he was sure that they had it. I said ok, I would like a short shelve shirt with a collar that buttons and shorts that are comfortable. Preferable an off gray or dark green. He said ok I'll see you next week.

Next week he came in with our linen and handed me my new lawn care outfits. They looked like they were brand new and weren't warn at all. I said WOW they look new and how much. He said $10.00 for 2 shirts and 2 shorts. You can't even go to Wally World and get them for that cheap. What a deal. I now have a better professional look much better than before.

Most of you can get in contact with your local linen company and see if they have used outfits for you to buy. Maybe if you need to supply your staff you might be able to get a price break due to the amount. Just look up uniforms in your telephone book or online and give them a call.

I bought 2 shorts and 2 shirts for $10.00. They have a plethora of used colors, styles and sizes. They look and feel brand new. If you wanted to have a look for yourself or crew maybe this is the way to go. I know that it would be too hot in some areas to wear but the look would be nice and professional. Maybe this can help some of you. It helped me."

The fear of getting too many lawn care customers.

Fear is an interesting topic. It is amazing how the fears we have can effect how we see the world and what we do in the world. A lawn care business owner brought up a great topic that has popped up in the past, leading me to think many lawn care business owners may share this fear. He wrote "I had a nightmare about gaining 1,000 lawn care clients. The problem was, I couldn't afford to serve them.

I didn't have the equipment, or the crew.

In my dream I wanted to serve all of the lawn care clients, I didn't want to lose any of them. I was afraid that they'd never think of hiring me again if I said no this time, so what happens?

I woke up…

Now imagine if the nightmare was true. In the Spring you send out 10,000 flyers and BAM, everyone calls you? Wouldn't that be worse than not having enough customers to fill your schedule?

I guess it's good to know what your maximum number of clients is. You never know what kind of trouble you'll have if you get too many. So you have to think, how many lawns can you mow (comfortably) in a day, multiplied by 5 days a week?

I'd say 11-12 customers a day, 5 days a week is good for ONE PERSON.

If you have a partner, 20 lawns a day, 5 days a week will be a walk in the park!

At first I did believe after my marketing, that everyone would call me. Though I simply said, 'I'll take what I can get, and leave the rest for other companies.'

The problem is, as I get bigger, saying no to potential customers will fill me with regret. Saying no might effect me later. When I can't take on more customers, they might remember me as "too busy" or the "no company" or most likely move on to a company who COULD take them.

Advertising comes in steps I guess. I hardly got any lawn care customers from my first attempts. The real gains I've gotten were from people seeing me work & walking up to me and asking for an estimate. Or referrals."

You bring up a really good point when talking about this fear. I think many entrepreneurs have a similar fear. It concerns them when they are doing their marketing.

Many times I have seen forum members post things like, 'I don't want to do too much marketing because I don't want to be swamped with customers.'

I think first off, if you can realize you won't be swamped with customers, you will be better off. Once you realize that, you will see you need to really overshoot your goals when you are marketing because no matter how many customers you think you will get out of what ever marketing campaign you are doing, ultimately you won't get anywhere near that amount.

This especially comes into play when a lawn care business owner is preparing to do some direct mail marketing to potential customers in their area. If you don't send enough pieces of mail out, you might not get any responses. I don't think it is possible to send out too many marketing pieces to your service area. At most we usually see a 1% to 2% response rate from direct mail or distributing door to door flyers.

Another lawn care business owner said "seeing is believing for most people. If you are mowing in an area where people can see you do a good job, they will come up to you.

This has happened to me many times. A person will normally walk up to me and say 'you mow my neighbor's lawn, can you come give me an estimate? I'm just down the street.'

Marketing in my opinion, can only build the base of what's to come in time. Everything will branch off from there.

One customer who initially got your flyer can refer you to their neighbor. The neighbor can refer you to their friend, etc.
Here is a list of which lawn care marketing methods have worked for me. Ordered BEST to WORST:

- People who have seen me work, who ask me for an estimate.
- Customers who have referred my lawn care company to their friends.
- Confronting people who look busy, and telling them I can mow your lawn for a price of $X.XX.
- Business Cards
- Flyers
- Craigslist."

If I still haven't alleviated your fears on getting too many lawn care customers, remember, you can always either take some of the new customers and stop servicing some of your lower profitable properties or you can simply say, at this moment we are back logged and we'll contact you as soon as a spot in our schedule is available.

How to get your first commercial lawn care customer.

If you are a newer lawn care business owner who hasn't made the jump yet to servicing commercial properties, you might be thinking, how do I land my first commercial lawn care bid. This questions seems to come up often and when I hear stories from those who made the leap I love to pass them on to you to help.

One of the members of the Gopher Lawn Care Business Forum wrote about his experience. "On a whim I just bid and won my first commercial job.

I noticed a really overgrown commercial property for sale and thought they may not have someone to take care of it. I was right and they were getting complaints from neighbors. My time estimate was right on so the job went well.

Now, if I want to continue, I know I need to invest in better tools of the trade. Thanks to this site for the information and templates, I followed one of them for my quote."

That is fantastic news! What have you learned so far from the experience? Would you have bid anything differently if you could re-bid it?

It is a former steakhouse, about the size of an Olive Garden.

"I learned that I can do the job with basic equipment and techniques but better tools would make it easier and faster.

In my opinion, I bid it perfectly. I ended up a half hour shy of my estimated time. I spoke to a friend that has an established lawn care business and he told me he would have done it for the same price but he could have done it for less if he needed the work."

There are a lot of new lawn care business owners that read the forum and I am sure they are wondering how did you get the bid lined up? Did you just walk in and talk with the manager or how did it happen?

"The restaurant is closed and the property is up for lease/sale. The owner is unsure if he will raze it or remodel.

Here is how I won this job:

1. I noticed a property for sale that is lacking attention.
2. I called the Realtor listed on the sign and ask to service the property.
3. The Realtor took my info, actually I emailed it to him.
4. Realtor passed info along to property owner.
5. Property owner's assistant contacted me and requested a quote.
6. I then had to find a suitable format for a quote (that I got it from the forum), I took another look at the property, visualized the work and put the quote in my own format.
7. In the meantime the Realtor contacted me and pressed me to get the quote in. The neighbors were complaining about the weeds.
8. I submitted my quote after settling on what I thought was a fair wage for my estimated time and materials.
9. The owner emailed me directly and accepted the quote. His assistant also emailed me and asked for a start date which I made a priority.
10. I completed the job quickly, took pics and, using a

template, created an invoice which I then emailed to the assistant.

11. I contacted the Realtor to let him know the job was complete. I also requested that he contact me when similar services are needed. He replied that he would and that I should keep in touch.

I see a niche market for servicing commercial properties w/o a long term contract…especially with businesses failing and new business growth stalled. A lot of properties are on hold and will fall into a state of disrepair without care."

What great advice and simple steps to take in order to submit a bid to a commercial property owner. I hope these ideas help you land more commercial properties as well.

How to use lawn care business bandit signs / yard signs.

Lawn care signs or bandit signs as they are called at times are an interesting and unique way to promote your lawn care business but do they work? Why are they referred to at times as bandit signs? That's because they are almost always illegal to use. Let's check out this question asked by a lawn care business owner when he wrote "does anybody have experience with putting out lawn signs on highway exit ramps and busy intersections to attract business?

If so, what are some things I may need to know? What kind of return should I expect from my advertising dollars if I go this route?

I'm asking this because I'm not at all satisfied with my return on the door hangers that I have been using. I have tried the door hangers and I'm not satisfied with my return no matter what neighborhood I put them in. I've even talked to people, shook hands, etc and gotten nowhere near where I'd like to be.

I need more business. I feel like I'm getting left behind and only getting occasional customers that other lawn care guys don't want.

I DONT' WANT THESE PROBLEM CUSTOMERS!!!

I want regular customers that keep me busy and don't cause problems."

One business owner suggested "here is some information on lawn signs. I used them a lot as a health/life insurance agent years ago....

1. In most counties they restrict or forbid temporary signage without a permit. Now you are not going to pull a permit for every sign (or any sign for that matter) so every now & then I'd get a call from the county saying these are illegal signs & that they removed some & those will be destroyed & that they recorded where others were. If I didn't remove them they would collect them & fine me per sign. (sometimes I went & got them, other times I did not) I never did get fined though. But the county will often pull them in a couple days so, I advise you to put them up on a Friday night & at least then they'll typically be up until sometime Monday or Tuesday.

2. Here is a bit of advise, have the signs made professionally but don't spend a ton of money on them. If possible keep it a simple one color design. Don't buy the stands. Go to local home improvement store & buy ladder wire. It will typically come in 12′ pieces. It's metal stuff typically used in between courses of cinder block when building homes to add reinforcement so it will be in the construction supply isle. Get a cheap pair of bolt cutters & cut the ladders into smaller sections to use as your stands. You can usually get about 4 stands per 12′ section. They are stronger & cheaper that way. And cheap is good since they will be removed by the county sometimes. Other signs will be taken by locals who want to cover your sign to make a yard sale sign!"

Another said "I do like yard signs , but you need to know how to use them.

I use them every weekend but I work close with code enforcement and find out were to put them and what days they work. I only put the bandit signs out on Sundays now because the code enforcers work Monday to Saturday here. This is for the city part of town. Now the county is a little easier, they rarely ever take my signs down. If fined the fee could be $500 per sign. But most of the time it's a smack on the hand.

Something else I do is get smaller yard signs and put them in your customer's yards. Not full time, move them around. People will see them while walking the dog or just driving by. Keep trying you will find something that works well for you!

One of the biggest and best advertising I have done was that I went out to all business owner in the area and talked to them about my business and put a stack of my business card on their counter with holder.
You will be surprised on how many people want to help and pass on referrals."

A third business owner said "I wouldn't recommend putting all your lawn care signs all out at once. I don't know where you live or how big it is but I would put a certain small test amount out.......look at the results. (see if they are mowed over or taken down, check them daily) Figure out the 'schedule' and post accordingly. If they mow Fridays then take them down Thursday. Put them back up when they are finished. I only have 3 up with my lawn care business. Two in customers yards and 1 waiting to be torn down on a side of the road."

After some experimentation here is what the lawn care business owner said who initially asked about the bandit signs. "I have updates. One customer has agreed to allow me to put one is his yard and I'm going to put some out on a busy parkway median on the way to where I have a few yards. I saw that they mowed the median yesterday. I went down that road Sunday and I noticed it wasn't cut, but saw the tractor w/ big mower attached parked on the side of a big hill. I figured they weren't cutting because it was Sunday and it was raining.

Monday it was all cut down. Gotta get out there and put out some signs, I'll probably start with about 5 because the parkway is kinda long. Maybe 2 at two different intersections and 1 strategically placed in median.

First night I put the signs out, I got a call the next morning and I have been getting calls steadily since I put the signs out. Somewhere around 3-5 a day. Some from the signs I put out on the busy parkway, others from signs I put in customers yards. One customer that has gotten me a lot of calls lives on a corner lot @ the entrance to a subdivision, I've gotten 4 or 5 calls from that sign alone!"

Lawn care business upsell idea - driveway sealing.

A question I get asked often is, what other services can I offer to make more money? I usually have a bunch of ideas to share with them but here is a great idea I hadn't even considered. One lawn care business owner wrote "yesterday I was out giving lawn care quotes.

We have had a few customers ask if we would seal their paved driveway, our response has been this is not a service we offer at this time however we will note you are interested should we decide to offer it.

I had two clients ask me about this today. I was at their homes for other work when it just came up.

As I was driving to find a milk shake I noticed two guys with a small truck spraying sealer on a paved driveway and decided to stop. They had a pretty simple setup. I asked for some business cards as we had clients asking and it was something we didn't do. I liked the job they did and we talked about pricing, subcontracting them etc.

They do this straight by the square foot, they roll around the edges of the driveway with a 16″ roller then spray. It is very quick to do this job but what a mess the back of their truck was.

They offered me a 20% referral which I think I will do for now, I don't think this is something that interests me due to the mess.

But as I was driving home I started looking at paved driveways, I think this could be another gold mine.

I think lawn care extends to property care. Any thing we can do to help the home owner and make a buck at, interests me.

Did more reading tonight on it and found this is a high profit margin service, seems like it is a fairly easy sale also.

The number one downside is the mess, I looked at a number of companies, pictures etc. The vehicles are a mess which I understand, it would be next to impossible to keep things clean and staff being what they are, it might not fit well with my image in yard care. Eventually even the inside of vehicles would be a mess even if we did use a trailer.

I called and spoke with the owner of this small company again last night, I received the names of two of his clients and called them to see if they were happy with the work done, that passed so I emailed him two of my clients and we shall see how this goes.

The issue with sub contracting in my experience is if there is an issue with the work, even though it's not your issue, your client will make it your issue as you referred someone. I have to take a chance and see how this goes, this could work for both of us."

What a fantastic insight! Maybe you could offer this service to your current lawn care customers or maybe you could find a company and sub-contract them out for a %. Experiment with both options and see which works best for you.

The trouble with lawn care business flyers.

Has your lawn care business handed out flyers to market your lawn mowing services? What kind of results did you receive? Were you happy with the results? One lawn care business owner talked about his frustration with handing out flyers and I got a chance to look into the potential reasons he was experiencing problems.

He wrote "back in June I printed up some lawn care business flyers and posted them along with everyone else's flyers at the grocery store, the laundromat, the beauty salon and local restaurants. The total number of calls in response to these fliers: Zero!

Nada. None. Zilch.

I do believe the problem is the same as with web ads. Nobody looks at them anymore. When you see them all the time you automatically block them out. Especially when you put your ad in the middle of 300 other ads. It's just sensory overload.

So far all of my referrals are from word of mouth of a happy customer.

I wonder if a news paper ad would generate more interest or if it's just another waste of time. Does anyone actually get a response from flyers?"

A second lawn care business owner shared "I too feel that lawn care flyers are pretty much a waste of time. A few years back they seemed to work better before the market was saturated with lawn care business owners.

Newspaper ads worked a little better but in my market there can be up to 50 ads at one time for lawn care and mowing service. Again market saturation.

Getting out there and working seems to be the best for me nowadays. People stop and ask for an estimate or other customers refer you."

A lawn care marketing business owner then shared his insight which might help shed some light on the situation. He wrote "How many flyers did you pass out?

I'm not pointing fingers at you, but I think it's important for all businesses (lawn care or not) realize that 1-2% response is about the best you will get. Don't get me wrong, some might get better, but using direct mail rates for a lawn care company, .5% is a good response.

Keep in mind this is a "response" rate and not a SALE rate.

So for example, if you passed out 1,000 lawn care flyers, the best you would get is 20 phone calls. How many of those calls you convert to sales depends on many variables.

I think the most important thing to consider with any marketing is… volume. But good volume is the key. If you want to target home owners, then using something like those mass mailed envelope of coupons where it goes to homes, apartments, condos, etc. may not produce the response you are looking for. Newspaper ads are the same thing. For every newspaper bought by a "potential" customer probably two are bought by people who would have no need for your service. BUT STILL… these are still effective sometime, but the response you get based on the circulation rate might not be what you're expecting.

You mentioned displaying flyers at the laundromat… I'm assuming you're in the lawn business. Think of the customers you have now, I would say that most have their own laundry room, and don't visit a laundromat.

You need to put your flyers, or ANY advertisement where it's most effective. Putting flyers/door hangers etc. at a single family home door or mailbox should get you the best response. It takes lots of time, but it's effective when done right. If you're lazy like me, use direct mail, it's costs more money because of the postage, but you'll hit the most amount of home owners in the shortest amount of time.

I've tried lots of advertising over the past 14 years, been part of a franchise, worked for the "big guys" and am now on my own, so I've seen all types of methods work and fail."

These are great points. You can print out 1,000's of lawn care flyers and if they don't get put into the hands of decision makers looking for lawn care services, you are wasting your resources. What you put on your flyer is just as important as who gets your flyer when you are looking for success.

Do lawn care business door hangers work?

What a great topic! Do lawn care business door hangers work? In early June a lawn care business owner had just put out 500 door hangers and didn't get a single call from them. Here is what he wrote "I just opened my new landscaping business. I got 500 door hanger out and I have not gotten a single call from anybody. Each door hanger had an offer for each customer who signs 1 year agreement $20 visa gift card and 10% OFF their 1st month. I just can not believe I have not got any calls yet. Also wanted to ask about how to make an offer for commercial such as (apartment complexes , shopping centers, restaurants ...etc). Should I mail them an offer, or what to do ? Thank you for you help"

Here are some of the suggestions that other lawn care business owners shared.

"I'm not too sure where your location is but here in the south our season is year round but it really picks up May 1st. If a customer wanted to change out with there current lawn care business they would have been thinking of this in March/April. Our season is in full bloom in May and the clients don't like to change unless there is a real problem with the workmanship.

Secondly, I don't really believe in door hanger because most people think what the heck is this on my door and rip it off and toss it in the trash. Word of mouth is great. If you have friends, family, co-workers ask them if you can do their lawn. Grab a couple and then you have an in when searching for more clients. They see your work and are impressed, then they ask you to take a look at their house and maybe you can get a job from it. Be more resourceful in what you can offer. Look at the house and see how many services you can offer them. Be resilient and good things will come."

"Regarding the landscaping door hangers, on average you can expect to receive about a 1-2% response rate. Handing out lawn care door hangers and making in person contact with the potential customer seems to be more effective because they tend to get a "feel" for you. I think this would be especially true for commercial jobs. I know if you were bidding on my property, I would like the face to face time much better than trying to discuss this via telephone."

"I don't recommend starting with commercial properties. Stick to residential. Person to person communication is key to getting clients.

Make business cards with a blank back. Knock on doors & sell your service. Ask them if they'd like you to give a free estimate (on the spot), if they say yes, write your estimate on the back of the card.

I also offer a referral program, the more customers one person gets me, the less they pay for lawn service. Try it out, forget gift cards, I tried that but it all really comes down to paying LESS for a service these days."

"I tried door hangers in neighborhoods where I already did work. Got some results but I think I got the work because of the current customers referral rather than the door hanger.

The best results I have received other than referrals has been the local newspaper!

My second best source has been handing out magnetic business cards. I get them for $9.95 to $19.95 per 50. Some printers will even give a coupon for 25% off your next order. Hand the potential customer a business card, it goes in the garbage. But, you hand them a magnetic business card it goes on their refrigerator.

I no longer post flyers. I keep some to hand out in person. If you put it in their hand they think they know you. You're not a blank face on the phone. I also work with real estate companies. I got them by offering to set up a display at their open houses.

I also give referral bonuses to my customers and real estate agents. 1 referral = a $10.00 gift certificates. 2 = $20.00, 3 = $30.00, 4 + $50.00, and 5=$100.00. This works. I do the lawn treatments for 4 agents now."

"In early June, you are starting too late for door hangers and definitely too late for commercial work.

Most people have their lawn care business service providers locked up for the season by now. You may get a client who is disgruntled with their current landscaper and wants a change. If I were you I would concentrate on other services. Get your foot in the door on a mulching or hedge trimming job. Give that customer your business card and remind them that you are a full service lawn care company and to keep you in mind for next season. This personal contact is much better than door hangers.

As far as commercial jobs start knocking on doors this Fall and early Spring. Most commercial accounts need to be in place weeks before the season starts. Find out who is in charge of grounds maintenance contracts and ask them if you can submit a bid. I Hope that helps."

"My door hangers were a bust too. Spent a lot of money for professional design, full color printing and distribution. Put out 1,000 and got 1 call that turned into a 1 time job for $175. It's all about getting jobs through people you know. Google adwords is by far the best advertising dollar I've spent. Don't give up and don't be too focused on getting weekly accounts. A lot of the weekly customers I've encountered are looking for the $15-$20 per cut, I won't do it. I have landed jobs doing clean ups for $175 to $500 and replacement of shrubs and bark ($75 - $200)."

Lawn care postcards to drop off as you drive by.

Have you ever found yourself out driving from job to job when you see a property that could really use one of your services? As you drive by it you think to yourself hmm if I could only get them as a customer. But what is the best way to promote yourself to potential lawn care customers as you are driving by? One lawn care business owner I talked to has found a solution that he shared with me.

He wrote "Here is an idea that has been working for us and working very well.

I have some full color post cards printed that look simply amazing. A few weeks ago I was driving with an employee and we noticed a lawn that was covered in dandelions, to the point there was no grass.

It struck me we should have a card along the lines that "We were driving by your property today and noticed ...., Our company would be pleased to provide services to help you out and as always our estimates are free. A complete list of our services is on the back of this card or visit our website at ....

So I had 500 cards printed, here are a few of the issues covered.

- Dandelions have taken over your lawn
- Weeds are taking over your lawn
- Brown patches in need of help

- Mold from trees on your siding
- Leaning trees you might want to have cut
- Driveway might need to be graded
- You have a pile of top soil you might want us to spread
- Save your back, we can spread that crusher run for you
- Brush seems to be taking over, we have brush saws
- Your front deck might like a pressure cleaning
- Their is water on your lawn, we offer drainage solutions

I know there are a couple more as I think we came up with 12. If I or my employees have time and notice something driving by a house, they will stop and give the owner a card or leave it in the door, it really works well as the prospect sees that we are paying attention."

That is very creative! Maybe you could highlight or check or even circle the services you think they could use too? To bring extra attention to them.

He replied, "I thought about that as it would have been cheaper than having cards printed for various services however I thought one card for each would look a little more professional. I know from studying my internet traffic reports, people are going to my website anyhow which lists everything we do.

This works well, our recent focus has been pressure washing decks and siding. I hired a full time employee with a vehicle to do only this service and it's working. Since we have staff at various sites every day, they know to look around and they either mention it to the customer and leave a card or they simply leave a card if the client is not home.

We find we are picking up a significant amount of business from neighbors, word of mouth and the lettering on our trucks and trailers.

I did a small excavation job for a lady yesterday, our city has over 300,000 people, she said I see your trucks, trailers and employees every where I go, you must me a big company and doing well which is why we hired you.

I laughed to myself and told the staff later. I don't consider us a big company. Our vehicles do get around and some of the staff like to wear their jackets outside work hours which is great. I was once told by one of our marketing people in another company, image is everything and I believe it is the case."

Are you offering organic lawn care services?

There has been quite a bit of talk about offering organic lawn care services on the forum lately. From what everyone has been saying, the profit margin on offering the service makes it worth while. Another great point is that you don't need any sort of chemical applicators license to do this so you could indeed get started offering these services today.

One of the lawn care business owners started the conversation off by saying "you really need to get into natural organic lawn care. I did a job this morning where I fertilized, enriched the soil, and aerated the lawn using an organic product.

My material costs were $102.00 and my labor was $30.00. Including travel I spent 2 hours. I bid the job at $408.00 ($24.00 per 1,000 sq. ft.). After material and labor I grossed $337.00 or $118.50 per hour!

I have 5 similar jobs for tomorrow. They are smaller lots but the same $24.00 per 1,000 sq. ft. price. I get 50% down with each order and balance on completion. Jobs I did last week led to me getting 4 of tomorrow's jobs. The results are pretty amazing and the neighbors are actually pre-sold.

I have only been using these organic products for a few weeks now and I am adding a service truck next week just for spraying!"

Another owner said "I was telling my better half about what y'all have been saying about this spraying deal. I told her that I think the organic sketter spray would sell pretty good around here. I don't think I could get what y'all have been getting as far as profit, due to the fact we have had so many factories closing around here in the past few years, a candy factory and a large tire factory closed down. Another factory is talking that they are struggling and are gonna cut back 300 jobs. But I still think it would sell good around here. I sure got my thumb out for this band wagon."

"This product sells itself and the results are striking and the performance tested. We are getting a tremendous amount of word of mouth jobs. I charge the same rate per 1,000 sq. ft.

Currently I keep two full time and one part time person spraying. A couple of weeks ago we added a four month spray program which I believe is necessary to get the maximum results from these organic products.

It costs so little to get into and the profits are light years ahead of mowing and it's fairly easy work. It does requires some self education and make sure you do so before you start selling. We run into organic gardeners on a regular basis and they will quiz us.

The big thing I get is 'many national companies advertise organic lawn care, what sets you apart?', I personally love this question. The products we use is 100% certified organic."

"Do products like these fall under typical restrictions? Do they require specific licensing? Or not since they are organic?"

"Both the EPA and the FDA classify these products as food sources. There are no restrictions or specific licensing required. I post the MSDA (Material Safety Data Sheets) required by OSHA on my website and carry copies in all my vehicles. I have been checked!

I offer a 4 part spray plan. I offer a 15% discount for repeat sprayings. $34.00 per 1,000 sq. ft 1st application and $28.90 per 1,000 sq.ft. and for subsequent applications. I also give a gift certificate for purchasing referrals. 1 referral=$10, 2= $20, 3=$30, 4=$50 and=$100.

Present customers are really going after the $100.00 card and the profit makes the referral 'gift' easy to give. And, I am checking to see if it could be used as an advertising deduction."

"Thanks for the info. I have been thinking of adding organic lawn care to my list of services. I already have the proper sprayers. There definitely is a market in my area for this. I am going to educate myself on this stuff."

Don't be afraid to hear the word 'No.'

Are you afraid of hearing the word no? Is it keeping your lawn care business from growing? This fear afflicts more of us than we would probably care to admit. A new lawn care business owner shared with us his insights as to how fearing the word 'no' had stifled his growth for some time.

He wrote us on the Gopher Lawn Care Business forum and said "I have been in the lawn care business since 1973 and it is still one of my passions of life. I have worked for large corporations and small landscapers and have taken every opportunity to learn as much as I can.

I now work for myself. I hope to continue learning from you folks and have no problems at all with sharing my experiences and knowledge with any of you. I have great customers and am looking to expand on services I offer and the neighborhoods I service in my area. I'm going to do this a little at a time in steps so as not to scare people off."

You have been in the business for quite some time! What do you feel about the differences between working for all those companies and running your own business? Any thoughts as to why you decided to make the jump and how you did it?

"I would suggest to all that I have NEVER been afraid to tell a lawn care customer or potential customer that I didn't know the answer to something, but I always made it a point to get back to them with an honest, sensible solution to problems they presented to me. It took me a long time to accept that some people can have differing views of things that will not agree with what you are presenting.

For the longest time, I was scared to death to hear "NO". I suffered economically, physically, and psychologically to keep from hearing that dreaded two-lettered word. I would suggest that we have to accept some failures in order to appreciate our successes. None of us wants to lose money in our daily endeavors, nor should we. I decided to go out and start my own because at a certain point, I figured out I can take my knowledge to the public and not be stuck or limited by my "boss's" imagination. The freedom to be my own representative out there in the world was too strong to ignore. I've gone back to work for other people from time to time but have finally settled on my independence and am truly enjoying myself. Yeh, I think I'll do this until I'm forced to retire."

With all of your experiences, what advice do you have for the new lawn care business owner who is trying to attract customers? What have you found that works and what doesn't?

"My advice to everyone would be to make up some flyers or have them made up for you. You can be as fancy as you can afford but be careful not to make it too long. Keep it short and sweet. Identify your services offered and maybe your service call policies, along with guarantees and licenses. We all have differing ideas about details but getting to the point is more a plus than a minus. You can always expand on what you are offering once you get in the door. Eyeball to eyeball is still the best way to sell yourself to anyone. I speak from experience, folks."

So if we can learn from his year of experience, it's that should constantly try to learn from others. Don't be afraid to hear the word no and to really sell yourself, get out there and talk to people eyeball to eyeball.

Targeting vacant lot clean ups.

Slow economies tend to drive people that once were employed into finding side work on their own. Sometimes this side work is offering lawn care. When too many people are offering lawn care services, the price in the area tends to drop. So what do you do?

This is the situation a member of the Gopher Lawn Care Business Forum found himself in as he shared with us his story and his new marketing angle.

He wrote "things are going a little better for me lately. I don't have any recurring weekly contracts, but I have landed a few clean ups. Weekly lawn mowing is just too cheap around here. The customers want to pay $100 a month. Maybe I'm just getting the lowballers or maybe the lawn care market is just over saturated with lawn care businesses.

My experiment with handing out door hangers has flopped. Posting on craigslist has been good to me as far as getting calls, but all the callers have been lowballers so far. My best paying work has come via search engine ad words. Pay-per click seems to work the best so far. I'm debating next on direct mail vs. newspaper ads right now. I'm also thinking of doing my own direct mail piece to all the real estate and property management companies."

This is very interesting! Who would you be targeting with your direct mail effort?

"The direct mail would be targeting new movers. Hoping to get the foreclosure buyers (with neglected landscaping), new to the area folks, new home buyers, etc. I can do a single mailing for about $0.42 per household.

The newspaper has a very wide reach, much less targeted. I worked for the paper before and the fact of the matter is, they produce calls. My concern is that 15 of my competitors are already in the service section. The ad runs about $165 to $220 a month. It's hard for me to justify the cost to be just another line ad in the paper with competitors above and below me. I do still have some pull at the paper so I might be able to negotiate placement.

Something else that is popular in my area is mowing vacant residential lots. Due to weed abatement laws they have to be mowed. I have seen some in my area already being mowed and that gave me the idea. I see a guy with a tractor offering this service. I think I can tough these jobs out with a heavy line trimmer/brush cutter and my high wheeled push week wacker."

That is a great idea. The average start up lawn care business may not be able to do such jobs because of underpowered equipment. Depending on the height of the lawn, a more powerful and specialized piece of equipment like your high wheeled weed wacker may be needed in order to make money on these jobs. This gives you a competitive advantage that I think you should jump on. Great thinking!

How to win over a property manager.

This is a very interesting topic. Lawn care business owners are always looking for ways to land commercial lawn care bids. But what's the best way to do it? There are many ways to go about getting close with property managers to win bids but there is nothing like hearing the inside scoop straight from a property manager himself. That is what I was lucky enough to hear in this discussion. A lawn care business owner had asked "my question is how to get commercial properties? Everyone tells me I have to go to them, they won't come to me. Before we get into this I would like to tell you about my business.

I started my lawn care business four or five years ago with about four accounts my first season and second season I got up to about ten. That's all I had for the next two seasons. So for this season I advertised with signs and that got me up to about twenty five accounts give or take. I now moved up from a 21 in push mower to a 36 in commercial walk behind. What my question is, is that I would like to expand into commercial businesses in my area because all I've been doing is residential yards. I'm wondering when to start looking for these commercial properties for next season and how to land them?"

Great question and here is some insight shared with us from a property manager. He responded "Hello, I am a property manager of 2 million sq ft. I was reading this and thought I would throw in a few thoughts.

The company I work for prepares it's budgets at the end of August beginning of September with final revisions in October. This is a little earlier than most, but not by much. Especially given today's economy, we are looking at every expense harder than ever before. One of the differences I did this year in accepting bid's/proposals was I wanted every item broken out. In the past I would ask for the total year number, number of cuts and what that number included. I put together a bid package outlining what I want, and then get the number as a whole.

This year I wanted every service provided broken out, ala cart. I am tailoring the service to my budget and cutting costs where we can. I am looking at everything from irrigation maintenance to fertilizer and tree trimming, trying to find small amounts that can be cut to make a difference. However small. Maybe this year I will only trim the tree's once and fertilize once instead of twice like last year. Not sure, but I need options right now.

I have met a lot of resistance from several contractor's telling me not to cut back on fertilizer or other services, but the fact of the matter is that the budget is so tight and the property incomes are so greatly reduced, every dime I can squeeze out has an impact.

Those landscape contractors that I invited to bid this year tended to get my attention about 6 months ago. Maybe once a month sending me an email or brochure after a phone call. I actually throw out the ones that got overzealous, but that's just me. I don't need a call every week. Once a month is fine. I have a lot of other things going on, but again, that's just me.

Insurance is a priority. I am in large scale commercial property management and all of my contractors are required to carry 2 million in insurance. We used to take 1 million, but now only 2 million is looked at.

I require terms also. Sorry, but my office, on average gets 100 invoices a day. We handle approx 10 million sq ft, so lots of things need to be paid. It's just not possible for me to cut a check the same day or typically even a week to get someone paid. We require all contractors to be on a 30 day invoice. Obviously we are good sized and a lot of smaller companies can turn invoices around faster, but if you want our work, you have to meet the terms.

Lastly, and more than anything I look at is references. I require, and call, references. Sorry, your brochure looks great, but I don't know you from Adam, so I need to talk to people that do know your work.

One final thing I would like to throw out there for thought- this year has been bad for commercial real estate and the forecast for next year is to be much much worse. I would caution you that there are a lot of real estate companies out there on the verge of closing and are having a hard time paying their bills, and for that reason may be making a fast switch because the place needs to be maintained, but they didn't have enough cash to pay the last guy. Just be wary of anyone making the "fast switch" right now. I am also seeing a lot of companies stretch those 30 day payment terms into 45-60 days.

Again, we are pretty good sized and I'm sure that's not what everyone here had in mind about commercial, but I just thought I would try to contribute."

What fantastic insights. Now that you know all this, you can take this information and use it to your advantage when trying to get the attention of a property manager.

Being on site longer improves your chances of selling more.

With many small lawn care businesses, the owners tend to feel there is more money to be made when you get in and get out fast. However as we will see in this discussion, offering more services than simply lawn mowing can help you be on the job site longer. The longer you are on the job site, the better your chances are of meeting neighbors and others driving by. These meetings can lead to adding new customers. One of the members of the Gopher Lawn Care Business Forum asked a question that kicked off this discussion "I thought of a neat idea for all of us. Everyone will state what services we offer & explain how you go about doing them. This will give everyone a clear idea on what services they might want to add to their business. I'll start.

Services I offer:

- Gutter Cleaning
- Weeding
- Spring/Fall Cleanups
- Topsoil/Fertilizer/Grass Seed
- Hedge Trimming
- Branch Cutting

The services I want to start:

- Grub Eliminating
- Aeration, $50.00 a yard is the cost around here.
- Driveway Crack Sealing (i'd add dye to the sealant to create the aged color)

The services I don't want to start:
- Gardening, planting…
- Tree Removal
- Anything that keeps me in the same spot for the entire day.

I don't like to stay in one spot doing a big job, which could bring me really nice income. I like lawn mowing because it's quick & keeps me moving, I tackle a lot more & it feels great. I do weeding, but personally I hate being at a job site for even more than 5 minutes. As for landscaping in general, even if I'm good at something, I just don't enjoy it. "

Another business owner said "I have to ask why you don't want to offer those additional services? Personally I love jobs that keep the staff at one location for the day or hours at a time, your percentage of profit for the job will be far larger than moving around. Factor in down time (travel with no pay) gas, maintenance, insurance etc. I personally found the big jobs pay a significant profit margin.

It also gives time for people passing by to see the work, it's free advertising and in our experience it pays big time."

Another lawn care business owner shared "I have to agree, generally speaking the longer I am at a job site landscape jobs (not mowing or fertilization) the more profit we make. No wasted travel time, loading and unloading equipment etc. Of course that is assuming the job was estimated properly."

A third said "I am trying to expand my business and the big jobs take me there. When I am on a job for the day, the neighbors take notice. I have business card holders that I put (I have velcro on my back truck windows and on the back of my business card holder). People stop to observe, take a card, and most often stop to ask questions. Having potential customers coming to you is far more productive than you going after them."

If we can learn anything from this discussion it's that staying on a job site longer, gives you a better opportunity to be advertising to the neighbors. The longer you are on site, the more neighbors you can meet and talk with. These talks can be a perfect way to line up new lawn care customers.

More secrets on winning over a property manager.

Here is the follow up conversation I had with a property manager on the Gopher Lawn Care Business Forum. He shared with me some really important insights you must know as a lawn care business owner if you want to win him or others in the industry over and get them to accept your bid.

I asked "I do wonder as you reflect back on your dealings with lawn care companies. Did any specific things some of them did really help them stand out and win you over? Or did it all just come down to who could do the job at the lowest dollar value?

Also, what kinds of things have lawn care business owners done that were an absolute waste of their time when they were trying to get your attention and market to you?

Could you also share with us the steps a lawn care business should take from how to initially contact the property management company to ultimately winning the bid? I am sure many readers would love to know how this works from your perspective."

He responded "first off, I don't think of myself as a price only customer. I am more than willing to spend the cash if the service is needed and worthwhile. That being said, we are looking at the bottom line more than ever and trying to figure out where we can save a few cents per sq ft. One of the reasons we are more "a la cart" this year is perhaps there are some duplications in services I am receiving from vendors. For instance, our current landscape maintenance company picks up all the misc trash around the property when they service the area. I love that, but I pay another company to do that three times a week, so is it possible for me to save a little if I ask you to cut that out? That's really where my effort has been in trying to cut costs.

As long as your price is reasonable, I am good with it. I know that sounds like I'm trying to cut corners but right now I am trying to compete with other landlords who are also trying to drop their costs to pass the savings along and get the few prospective new tenant's out there attracted to my property. Maybe this year I will plant annuals instead of every quarter replacing the entrance flowers etc. Those are the price issues I am addressing.

I've tried to think of some things that have/have not worked in getting my attention, but honestly, I have to say consistency, professionalism, you definitely need to show professionalism. No jeans and t-shirts and follow up. Being consistent in your calls to me, or your follow up email is important. A lot of it, sorry to say, is right time and place, and if you are consistent about reaching out to me, you will be there at the right time.

I'll also throw out one of the best things I have had a landscape company do for me. After every service call to one of my properties, I get a check list showing what was done, what needs to be done (along with costs) and when the next service call will be. That helps give me a picture of whats going on, so if I am asked any questions, I have the answers already and don't need to make a call to find out. "

What great advice. To round out the conversation another lawn care business owner jumped in and shared with us what has worked for him when trying to land commercial accounts. He said "the best thing to do is get out and talk to managers/owners face to face. Start up a conversation and ask if they are accepting any new bids for their lawn care and landscaping services. You will be amazed at how many business owners/managers are unhappy with their current lawn care company. Most businesses already have a lawn care company, so be prepared to not get a lot of commercial accounts the first year you go after them. If the business is not happy with their current lawn care company, they will usually be more than happy to let you know when their contract is up. Take some notes: What they expect, what the are unhappy about, and WHEN THE CURRENT CONTRACT ENDS.

Keep in contact with the people in charge (stop in and say hi/send a card around the major holidays) and submit a bid a couple weeks before the contract is about to end. Also have your act together: Company shirts, professional letterheads business cards etc., clean cut appearance (present yourself as a business owner, not just a guy that cuts lawns), and have your insurance in order. Hope this helps.

Remember a business wants to hire a professional company, not a guy in a truck with no insurance that doesn't pay taxes."

Sell more landscape services by staying put.

Why travel around so much when you can sell more staying put at the same location. You may not think you are missing out on potential upsells until you read this. One of our Gopher Lawn Care Business Forum members shared with us his view on staying put and making more on upsells. He wrote "I wanted to say it is 100% clear to me that we need to stay on job sites as long as possible and I have two very recent examples.

A customer contacted me and wanted some brush cleared and a small driveway put in for his camper. I met with the client, it was a simple $1,200 job.

We talked and walked around. As I look up I notice four large trees in the back leaning, I think to myself there is another $800, so I ask, do those trees concern you that are about to fall and hopefully not on someone? He said yes, he tried to cut them but then called a company and they wanted $1,500. He thought it was too much and declined. I said we would do it for $800 as our gear can go right into the area and chip the branches on the spot savings probably two days of time. Needless to say we got the job.

So as I am grading the small driveway, a neighbor comes over and asks how much to regrade my driveway? I say $200.00 to grade and roll. Long story short we picked up 8 jobs all on this street. The beauty of it all is that I don't have to move the gear at all.

At another location, we picked up 5 more excavation jobs, another starting today. When it's all said and done it is almost

$100,000 in work and we will never get it done this year.

The private gated community I do a lot of work at, is another example. People in these communities talk and we now provide total property care for four of these communities off the same street and another 9 from people right on the main road that are not from a community.

There is far more profit staying put. Transportation had always been an big expense issue for me but not anymore. There is enough work in this area to keep a good sized crew busy 6 days a week. I made arrangements with a homeowner to keep gear in his garage as he doesn't use it, in turn I will offer him free spraying, my cost is next to nothing and the security there is top drawer.

Point being, people see you once or twice at a site they just notice you, when they see you there for a period of time they take notice and wonder what is going on, it pays and pays well. Try to get jobs where you can really shine at what you do and stay there as long as the client has projects and money."

This made me think and ask "we have seen many different business viewpoints on here in the past. Some feel comfortable with point out issues on a property and offering to resolve them while others feel they don't want to be pushy and try to upsell any additional services. Some feel it is better to just do the job you have been asked to do and leave.

Do you feel this is something you had gone through in the past? Is there a process here of growing where at first you are not comfortable pointing out issues, but as you get more comfortable and confident in what you do, it comes easier?

What advice do you have for the business owners who sit there and read this thinking it's too pushy to be suggesting these upsells?"

He responded "here are a few ways to look at this. I do not hard ball sell. I can't stand anyone doing it to me and I won't do it to others.

I would bet 99% of the time the homeowner doesn't even realize we offer the service for something other than why they called me. I hear this all the time, Oh you do that??? I bid and almost always get it. To me, I am offering a solution to a problem, not trying to sell and get my hands deeper in the project.

My sales approach is very….hard to explain. It's almost buddy like. I befriend the homeowner quick which makes them comfortable, suggest we do things in stages. Most times they want it all, some agree do this then in xx weeks come back and do this next part, works every time for me.

My opinion, if you are in this business to make money, then do it. Look outside the box of simply mowing and trimming, there is a pile of cash to be made and a lot of people will be happy including you. If a person is afraid to sell or approach a customer with an additional offering and they want to make money, take a course to get you there.

I have never been afraid to upsell, why would we be? All the homeowner can do is say thanks but no thanks. Educate them on what it is you can do. If they say no, good lord it's not the end of the world. Even if they say maybe later as cash is tight, fine, at least they know and they will not forget. Raise you bar a little higher and make the jump, you can do it."

Performing landscape projects in stages can help sell them.

In a discussion on the Gopher Lawn Care Business Forum, we talked about how breaking landscape projects down into sections can really help you sell larger projects. If the customer knows that at anytime they can say ok this is enough or if they feel their budget is shrinking to pay for the landscape project, they will feel more in control when they know it's not an all or nothing deal.

I asked on the forum by offering landscape jobs in stages do you feel this allows you to build a rapport with the customer? So they don't feel like they are committed to a high value contract if they are not liking the results?

So they feel they can basically call an end to the project at any time and maybe that control over the job, even if they don't exercise it, empowers them and makes them want you to fulfill their dreams of a perfect landscape?

One of our members responded by saying "I have two thoughts, first if it's a good sized landscape project, doing it all at once is not good for anyone. If it's done in stages the client can change their mind along the way and add or take away things. It's good for us too as I don't like a crew on a site for more than a week. It's too much resources, however there are always exceptions.

You also have to keep in mind customer finances. If I give them a quote to do a landscape job of say $20,000, they will have sticker shock. If I say look, here is how we break this project up into four individual projects and let's both see how things go. First part will cost you $5,000 and here is what it will include, when we are done let's talk about stage 2.

This may not work for everyone but it works for me."

What is your view on not wanting to stay on-site for longer than a week at a time?

"I feel it's a long time to be at one location. In my head for some reason I like to move after a week but we will not leave any site until the job is finished and the customer smiling. It's hard to schedule work when you have jobs that go on and on. We had maybe 8 this year where we were there two weeks or more. I have found the staff also tends to get bored with the same site so I will switch some of them out after four days leaving at least 2 on the site at all times that have been there at least two days. By then they know everything that is going on. Sometimes however the client takes to a crew and doesn't want me to do this so I don't, that has happened at least three times."

Looking unsafe can get your lawn care company fired.

You may not think at first glance a lawn care customer pays much attention to the safety precautions you either take or ignore when working on their property, but they do. People keep track of when you take trimmer guards off or mower guards. They know what can happen when these devices are taken off too. You can get hurt, you can hurt somebody or you can damage property. Nothing drives a customer crazier than to have a window broken on their house or see that their new car was damaged all because you took off a safety guard.

They also know that if you get hurt on their property, even because of something you did to disengage a safety device, in the end you can sue them and collect on their home owner's insurance policy.

I bet many lawn care business owners don't consider this can play a factor in whether they will be rehired or not in the next season. No home owner wants a contractor hurt on their property. Those who show safety comes first on the job site are the ones that project professionalism. Those who don't look like amateurs and no one wants to hire an amateur.

Take a moment and ask yourself a few questions. Are you wearing a uniform or just jeans and any old t-shirt? Do you wear ear protection and eye protection? Do you wear boots or sneakers? Does your equipment have all the safety features still attached?

There is a reason why a police officer wears a uniform. It's so he stands out from everyone else and you immediately recognize he is a professional. When you look professional, you will stand out too. You improve your chances of being hired and you can potentially command a premium for your services.

A member of the Gopher Lawn Care Business Forum added a personal experience he had that allowed him to pick up a new lawn care account for the next year. He wrote "I see ZTR mowers on sites all the time and they are flying around. However clients actually do not care for this even if it's not their property. This is actual feedback I've had from talking to customers and I have to agree. Mowing fast has the potential to cause more problems. It's better to mow at a moderate speed and do a good job.

I picked up another mowing contract yesterday even though mowing season is finished. Why? Well the previous lawn care company that was doing this ladies property didn't wear safety gear and she said they had removed the guards from the trimmer. She was upset by this and didn't want them hurt on her property."

Another lawn care business owner shared "I couldn't agree more with your experience of showing concern about mower speed, safety, and attention to detail. It just looks so much better. My mower carries a pair of fire extinguishers on the roll over bar. It's an attention getter as some have noticed. Along with eye & ear protection the most important item of equipment to me are the dust masks I wear, when ever temperatures allow, while mowing and shredding as chemical applications could be hot for days.

I had a dear friend who was a weed chemical applicator in the yard and property biz for many years. He died several years back from a cancerous tumor he felt was from his occupation. Attention to details along with wanting to be the best has helped me stay booked all summer."

Lawn care businesses are always looking for ways to stand out from the pack and here are a bunch of great ways to do it. Look professional, act professional and reap the rewards of running a top notch lawn care business.

Free lawn mowing for single moms?

We talk a lot on the Gopher Lawn Care Business Forum about how when you do something good for the community, you can get a lot of attention. Especially when you let the media know what you are doing. In a recent article I read, it talked about a lawn care business owner who was offering free lawn mowing for single moms. It made national news, but was it worth it? That is the questions I asked and I got a lot of great responses on it that I wanted to share with you.

- "I don't mean to be a wet blanket, but this is a one time promotion gimmick. I remember back in the late 60's (showing my age) when a man sold everything he had and invested it in the lottery. He spent almost $60,000.00. He won about $12,000.00.

A Magazine Gave him the "Biggest Loser of the Year Award". They also gave him the "Biggest Winner of the Year Award"! Although he lost $48,000.00, he received over $100,000.00 in "guest appearances" on shows like Johnny Carson. He did it, and it was big news and was in demand and he profited from it. He had just received his masters in business marketing degree and he "leaked" his story to the national media. His "calculated" plan made him a lot of money, but it was a one time shot. Anyone following his lead, did so without getting the needed publicity!

What this lawn care business did was a marketing act of genius, but it's just not repeatable. It's already been done and therefore not news.

Although 'single moms' are sometimes very needy, there are other groups that don't get nearly as much governmental support.

Seniors who have lost their spouse and disabled Veterans come to mind. My wife is a pediatric critical care nurse and also a certified forensic nurse. She is always volunteering my services to sexual assault and domestic violence victims. I give discounts to veterans and special discounts to spouses left behind and especially to disabled vets. I don't seek publicity but I do make some very good friends along the way.

Community service builds a quiet reputation. Respected and remembered."

- "I've always believed being entrepreneurs gives us special privileges (and special responsibilities). We meet many members of the community and our eyes are opened to people who genuinely need a helping hand.

I was involved today with a group who helps disadvantaged widows in the local community. The lady we helped today is elderly and on social security. Her roof has been leaking for a few years and she does not have the wherewithal to have it fixed. A group of 12 of us did a complete tear off and re-roof today… completely free and no gimmicks.

Though my intent was not to benefit from the work I did today, I ended up making some amazing contacts in the local community. It always amazes me how kind deeds always seem to benefit both receiver and giver."

- "This is kind of my dilemma. I do free cuts for elderly and disabled people that can't afford it. I get accounts from word of mouth as they are always telling friends and neighbors how I help them. Something bothers me about telling a news person about it, even though I could really use more accounts and things are hard now. My intentions started by just trying to help someone, but when it started getting me business, well, I guess my motives aren't so "pure" sometimes. Its kind of like putting a hundred dollar bill in the offering basket at church and then telling everyone how generous you were. I may not be explaining it well, but its kind of a moral dilemma I suppose. If I'm helping people out so I can make more money, it takes something away from it don't you think? Then again, people in need are still getting their yards mowed for free, and the more accounts I have, the more I can afford to help even more people."

- "The single mom thing is out of the question for me. 90% of my business is single moms. There's a sort of "man pride" in taking care of your own yard, like changing your own oil, so homes with a man are a lot harder to come by. Instead of the single moms, I would choose to help elderly and the disabled without the extra income because they really don't have a choice other than have a family member come help. With my first free yard, it was that family member that paid me to do her own yard right after I took it over. The key is having someone refer you to someone in need.

At first, instead of advertising in the "household services" section of craigslist, I put an ad in the "free" section looking for people. I did get 7 referrals, and 3 people that referred wanted me to mow their own yard for money, but I also got 2 people asking to mow their own yard for free, and in nice neighborhoods, and I was too skeptical to reply. Everyone's going through tough times and I'm not going to mow an able body person's yard for free because of a layoff or something. I decided to stick to referrals.

The best way to avoid being taken advantage of is having people refer others in need to you, and not "volunteering" themselves. I got stories of recent widows in their 80's who spent their life helping other people, etc. I'm in this business so I can provide for my kids and I, and to give me the free time to be with them as much as possible, but when a little old lady is shaking my hand crying, and saying that I'm the angel she's been praying for (those were her exact words) there's no question I'm doing the right thing. There are just lots of issues to balance when offering free service."

Lawn care marketing idea for the Fall.

If you are trying to promote your Fall yard leaf clean up and gutter clean out services but find going door to door takes too much time. Putting flyers in mailboxes is also a problem because it's illegal and the Post Master can fine you. Well what about this? What if you got a whole bunch of these tiny lawn signs that are orange and look like pumpkins. You could go through neighborhoods and stick into the ground right near where the driveway meets the road to minimize distribution times?

It could really cut down on your distribution times. You could also throw in some kind of offer to give the potential customer a free pumpkin when they call for a free quote.

It's something different. It would stand out and it should not cost much at all for printing.

The front of the sign could have a message of offering yard and gutter cleanups.

While the back could offer a free pumpkin with everyone quote.

Cheaper price on lawn care in hopes of future work?

Have you ever been on a site to give a lawn care estimate and sensed there was plenty more work to come your way if you were able to land this account and develop a working relationship with the property owner? Did you take this into account when you gave your estimate price? Was it lower than you would normally have charged or would you never give a cost break in hopes of future work? This is a discussion we had on the Gopher Lawn Care Business Forum with a lot of great insight.

One lawn care business owner wrote "the most recent time when I implemented this strategy was with a local private community that had a grub issue. I low balled the association president's property. His place alone was about $8,000 in work. I quoted him $5,200. I then picked up all 6 homes plus a common area. Each property had their own issues and I made up for the low ball quote plus I picked up total property care for three years.

Having vehicles parked on site with a lot of gear was a marketing strategy I was counting on to work and it did. I now have four private communities on this same road, all within a 2 minute drive of each other.

We finished 800 feet of drain and regraded a 2,000 foot road yesterday for one customer. They have had 6 companies in four years try and fix their road. It had never been done properly. The customer sent an email to me last evening and said they have never seen such quality and detailed work and felt they now have the best looking road in the area.

Not only that, but this one new owner wants his lot cleared for a retirement home. The lot is 7 acres. We will clear a road into it, build the road then clear for the house. This job will run $30,000 to $40,000, it's quite a spread in price however there are a lot of variables and the owner agreed. We will start some this winter if there is not too much snow and finish next April/May.

If we want our foot in the door sometimes there is a cost to pay, in any business. The door could be someone that we could make money off from referrals, could be an area we want into or it could be that business is slow and we want to simply show our stuff.

A one time mow, clean up or whatever can lead to a lot of possibilities, some will work out and some will not, for what it's worth don't get hung up on the one's that don't work out and don't be afraid to do it again, we have to take certain chances. I was going to say risk but there is no risk in breaking even or losing a few bucks if you have a plan. A plan in this case would be having a chance to prove what you can do.

I understand some readers may be living hand to mouth due to a tough year, I have been there too, however I always tried hard to keep my chin up and do whatever it took to get the ball rolling."

Another business owner shared "I think you have to really read the situation & feel out the potential for future business to make the decision on a case by case basis.

When I first started my lawn care business up, a real estate investor who had 30 some residential properties called me because he had them listed with a property management company to get them rented. He didn't like the price he was paying or the quality he was getting from the lawn service vendor the management company used. He wanted someone else to do the work on just his homes (30+) whenever they were vacant, though the paper work would go through the property management company.

The price he was paying did seem a bit high, but he was also very concerned about the poor quality he had been getting. I gave him a site-unseen per property per cut price for one month, which gave me time to show him my quality & to see each property. It was a basic break even deal for 1 month but I figured it could lead to more work & it was better than driving around to estimate all those properties & possibly not getting any of them.

Well my initial rate was a bit low & the management company called me to let me know that they thought I was nuts & they didn't want me to think I could win over all of their business. They said 'we've been with our lawn guy for years & we are not changing just because your a little cheaper, so please don't sell yourself short for this one investor.' I said I am not & that's fine, I can respect that & that I knew what I was doing.

At the end of that 1st month I rebid each property for the investor & retained the work at a fair price. By the end of third month the management company started calling me for odd jobs or overgrown lawns the other guy didn't wanna touch. I stated I'll clean em up if I get to maintain them for you. I wasn't going to do the hard part so he could make the gravy. They agreed.

Inside of six months the companies Realtors & property managers were all apparently talking about how much better the yards I maintained looked than the other guys work & my rates were better! I won over the whole account & maintain it still today. They have also referred countless new home owners, tenants, & a couple other property management companies to me. The money I didn't make that 1st month seems laughable now doesn't it?"

Help! My lawn care marketing isn't working!

It's one of the most frustrating things to have to deal with as an owner of a small lawn care business, when you spend money on marketing and nothing is working. It can make you feel like you are in a ship that is sinking and no matter what you do to bail the water out, it comes in faster and faster. That is the problem a member of the Gopher Lawn Care Business Forum was dealing with when he wrote "I don't get it. I have put up lawn care flyers, handed out business cards, put ads on free internet ad sites and the local papers yet still I sit here with no calls at all. Several weeks have gone by with no calls at all. This is getting depressing. Is this the economy, am I doing something wrong? I want to suck all my marketing money back because I feel stupid paying for marketing when its not even getting my calls for quotes or anything."

One lawn care business owner wrote "how often do you stop and talk to a customer who may have a lawn or other issue you could fix and explain how you could cure the problem for them? When you see another provider at a place and let's say their quality doesn't meet yours, do you ever talk to the home owner to see if they are satisfied? Very, very few people will come to you unless one of their friends have told them about you, you need to go to them."

He responded "I don't do any of that but it may not be a bad idea. I have thought about walking around and knocking on doors whose yards are in despair. I'm not sure I would feel right trying to steal a client away from someone else by waiting until they leave and seeing if the customer is satisfied. Maybe it's a last resort but I am not sure I feel good about that."

I then asked if that is really stealing a customer or is that giving the customer a choice and a member suggested "take this for what it's worth. I am in this to make money, if it was a neighbor who mowed a lawn across the street and I knew I would do a better job I would be across the street and I would get the account. This is business my friend, people are not going to track you down.

By dropping cards on properties that needed a service that we offered, I would estimate it generated me well over $200,000 in business this year, that is not pocket change.

Not being critical but step out of the box, up to the plate and hit a few home runs, the first few might be awkward but if you want the ship to come in, don't wait go after it as it's there waiting for you."

Another business owner shared "don't limit yourself to problem yards (those in disrepair or the guy fighting with his lawn mower).

Target nice yards too. Prospective clients with nice lawns know how much work it takes to keep them nice. They are proud of their lawns and willing to pay a good price to keep them looking good.

Talk to them. If you're just starting out, ask what their secrets are. If they do the work themselves, point out areas where you can be of service (pulling weeds, raking leaves). Once your foot is in the door, and you prove yourself, you can turn them into regular customers.

It's a mistake to only target bad yards. Remember: Great customers beget great customers."

I asked what is better though, targeting nice yards or messy ones and I got this opposing view. "If you want to make money and get your name on the street fast, start with the lawn from hell and turn it into a golf course, I have done it many times which is why our growth is nuts this year.

I am not interested in a customer with a very nice looking lawn, a nice landscape or a very nice driveway. I feel it is wasting my time and theirs as I would be shocked if they would even talk to me and if it's not broke they won't fix it.

The reasons I have found most lawns are messy or need help is because the homeowner has not used the right products. They generally they do not overseed. They had grubs or cinch bugs at one point and didn't take the time to find out how to bring it back. Poor quality lawn cutting can have a negative effect as well as there might be trees that have fallen, the customer had a quote but it was too expensive.

The target market for me is middle and upper middle class home owners. Generally speaking they just do not have time but they would like to have their porperty look nice.

If a yard is full of junk I would never stop, the only clean up jobs we do is leaves, branches and trees."

Mow a neighbor's lawn and get a new account?

Have you ever been out mowing your customer's property and looked over at the neighbors to see their lawn could use a cut too? Did you ever decide to cut their lawn? Well a member of the Gopher Lawn Care Business Forum told us a little story about what he has been up to and how he landed his latest account with this new marketing technique.

He wrote "It's been a while, here's an update! I invested in great new equipment this season. An new chainsaw, trimmer, hedge trimmer and blower. I got an 8hp chipper/mulcher to reduce piles of sticks everywhere. A compressor and tools for removing mower blades. A bench grinder and a 2008 12′ x 6″ aluminum trailer!

See how successful I've become? LOL OK, most of it was from a "business loan" from Grampa, but it sure looks like I'm successful! I just got a new account yesterday and did some tree work for her too. I still do 5 yards for Realtors that have vacant homes they're listing too.

This week's focus: commercial accounts! My Realtor buddy is working on some leads for me with properties he has connections with. I got a list of 130 apartment and condo association addresses and phone numbers I'll be visiting / calling starting next week. It seems to me that it shouldn't be much harder getting a commercial account than a residential right? Well, a little, but when you figure that one good commercial account could equal many residential accounts, it's time well spent.

Another thing I've been doing is making it a point to talk to neighbors when I mow. Last week when I finished a yard, I mowed the neighbors too and left a card. That new account I got yesterday? Yep, you guessed it, it's from the free mowing I did! Things are coming around, slowly but surely."

That is fantastic! This could fall under the topic, barring risk there is no reward. If this works for one client, can you imagine if you promoted it to other neighbors of your customers? You could end up creating a very tight lawn care customer route. Good job in being so creative.